POSITIVE
MINDED
PEOPLE

POSITIVE MINDED PEOPLE

Inspiring stories of overcoming adversity for living a more positive life

BENNIE MAYBERRY

Calvin Witcher	Jeremy Witcher
Giana Cicchelli	Noah Alvarez
Kim O'Neill	Michelle Paquette
Drew Bensen	Jaime Aplin

Witcher Publishing Group

POSITIVE MINDED PEOPLE - Inspiring stories of overcoming adversity for living a more positive life. Copyright © 2017 by Calvin Witcher

Published and distributed by Witcher Publishing Group.

Contributing Editor: Jeremy Witcher
Editorial Review: Shell Taylor
Editorial Insight: Kim O'Neill
Cover Design: Lamont Johnson and Calvin Witcher
Interior Design: Calvin Witcher

This book may be purchased in bulk for educational, business, fundraising, or sales promotional use. For Information, please email info@witcherpublishing.com

Publishing consultation, support, design, and composition by Witcher Publishing Group. www.witcherpublishing.com.

Library of Congress Cataloging-in-Publication Data

Trade Paperback ISBN: 978-0-9995309-0-0
E-book ISBN: 978-0-9995309-1-7

Because of the dynamic nature of the Internet, any web addresses or links contained in this book may have changed since publication and may no longer be valid. The views expressed in this work are solely those of the author and do not necessarily reflect the views of the publisher, and the publisher hereby disclaims any responsibility for them.

All chapters are the sole thoughts and viewpoints of the respective co-author based on their ideals and individual expertise and experience. Any principles and philosophical information should not be considered medical, legal, mental health advice or otherwise. All references to external information are common knowledge and should be treated as such.

Witcher Publishing Group - rev. date: 10/25/2017

Witcher Publishing Group
WitcherPublishing.com

Dedication

I want to dedicate this book to my mother, Precious Mayberry. You loved hard, right from where you were, and I thank you for that. I also dedicate this book to my best friend Calvin Witcher. Without your help, this would not have been possible and would have never been a reality. You are honestly a brother to me and I want to thank you for guiding me through this process. And, to all authors and Positive Minded People, may this group continue to be a platform for all of us to share our own stories of triumph and create new ones along the way.

Bennie Mayberry

Contents

Acknowledgments

Thank you to every beautiful soul that reads this book. May the experiences, that are expressed in this book, be a source of empowerment for your life. Get ready to embark upon a new journey in your life that you will never forget.

Introduction

No story is too small or too big. Every story is worthy of sharing. There are always storylines in our life that we're not proud of and that make us vulnerable to share. Regardless of what our story is, it's only by telling our story that we experience freedom. And, from that freedom, comes self-discovery, which in turn allows each of us to be agents of freedom for others.

As founder of Positive Minded People, this group has been a platform to vocalize my most challenging and triumphant narratives in my life. Most see me as this happy, goal-aggressive, loving, and kind person. Most also don't know that for over 16 years, I dealt with depression, drugs in my family, extreme poverty, and self-hatred so deep that I tried committing suicide three times.

I didn't find my "happy" place by accident. I found happiness intentionally. And, the authors in this book are no exception.

Over the next nine chapters, you will have a chance to

connect with other members of Positive Minded People.

For months, these authors had the incredible charge to relive some of the most challenging moments that changed their lives. Tears were shed, emotions were felt, but through it, new life-changing discoveries and perspectives were gained. This book became the platform to share those stories and it was a vehicle for healing.

In this book, we share stories of suicide, starting over from failed relationships, LGBT issues, self-acceptance, addiction and everything in between. No rock was left unturned. The ability to live a more positive life in the midst of adversity is achievable. Being positive is not a coping skill. It is a real tool to redefine experiences in order to produce a better outcome. It helps you show up differently. Positivity keeps you going from within yourself when every reason around you tells you to quit.

Since 2011, when I started Positive Minded People, we've hosted hundreds of events and I've met thousands of people along the way. There are stories that have changed my life, yet we're left untold. So, by creating this book, and the books that will follow, it is my prayer that your story be told.

Stories have a way of impacting and inspiring people. They serve as a reminder that you can understand yourself, learn from the experience, overcome the past, and make something good out of the entire process. Your story is a memorandum that serves to help you realize that although life is not always easy, it's not impossible either.

I want to thank all the members of Positive Minded People who have taken part in this journey. My hope is that you receive inspiration through this book. Now that you know how to use adversity as a catalyst for change, I hope you will continue to share your story to the world.

It's your story, and it's your time.

CHAPTER 1

HEALING WITHIN THE PAGES OF YOUR STORY

Noah Alvarez

Relationships are naturally complex, and I've decided that not only can I live with that, but I truly enjoy exploring the deeply rich textures that make up the intricate crochet-woven tapestry of the relationships in my life. Taking the time, six years to be exact, to clear deeply rooted trauma has given me the divine opportunity to see the beauty in others' journey toward self-love and inner peace. In hindsight, I see how observing and embracing the journeys of people I love without judgement has been the greatest element of healing for me. It is, paradoxically, the one thing I desired to receive most from everyone else around me.

It is my belief and experience that human beings encounter opportunities to heal familial wounds through their nonfamilial relationships. Those storylines give us the jolt back into our birthing experience, and allow us to make conscious choices on how to call forward memories that are hidden deep within us, from a place of mindful orchestrator rather than helpless victim. Something like relational Deja vu.

When a lover disappoints us, it's the perfect time to go within and relate into some of the other relationships we hold sacred. Regardless if our surface interactions with loved ones are love-filled or stress-inducing, it's important to acknowledge the "why" we hold on to painful experiences like luggage we're dragging behind us, rather than let them pass through like soft wind on our faces. How we interact with the experience of a friend betraying us, is a great mirror to how we hold our expectations of loved ones' closer to us than the actual body, mind, and soul of the people we feel so impacted, so distracted, and even restricted by.

When I was asked to contribute to this book, I knew that there were handfuls of stories of suffering, loss, and healing to choose from, to share to an audience who may be seeking a pathway toward greater harmony and well-being. As I really sit with the offering that was presented to me to contribute in this way specifically, it isn't one memory from my past that comes to me - rather I'm reminded of a constant energy that followed me through many of the painful yet purposeful experiences that have shaped the man I am today. The energy that I'm speaking of has been with me since I can remember; like a friend who does not speak using words, rather it connects to me like an invisible floating mirror - allowing me to center myself through the reflections of others and even within their actions and experiences as I am privileged to be a witness to their unique yet familiar unfolding. I sit with the task of sharing a message in the hopes of inspiring something true and potent within you. As I reflect on what to share, I can't escape the mirror that you are to me, even now as I write these words where I am, and you read them, from where you are. The unfolding is in the knowing that we are already connected. The story can only be embraced if you trust me. In this, I extend my hand to you now.

There is indeed something here, now, that is connecting us. It isn't the anecdotal lost scenes from my childhood, or even a shred of wisdom to guide you into a new season or your "due season" for love and happiness. What is present in this moment (if you choose to be fully here now) is the sameness and deep togetherness that our individual growing pains have already caused, outside of the construct of time. You and I both know pain, and that one thing is certain.

It is in my own attempt to tell a portion of my story, that my mind and heart are most deeply entrenched in the energetic resonance of your story. I feel it now, and though your story has not escaped your lips nor has it hit my ears, I feel your sameness... as you have found these pages, and in this we have found each other right where our pains (and our pleasures) have positioned us. Our stories have travelled long ways to bring us here, separately and together. For better or worse, my pain has operated in the same way your pain has, in bringing me to this very moment with you. Like two oak trees firmly planted, side-by-side; our branches may never touch as we grow and elevate toward the sky through the seasons and winds of change, but our roots that surely run deeper than our branches are high, are intimately connected, by design. It is intentional for us to trust each other's pain, through the telling of our stories.

So, now that we have come to the comfortable conclusion

that space and time are not mutually exclusive determining factors in connection, as I am confident you will agree, I can only hope it is not too forward of me to also impose on you the suggestion that the only reason for you to take in a piece of my journey, here, now, is to be reminded of the healing that the storyteller within you is capable of facilitating over the surface-area of your own being. The beautiful thing about relationships, though they are indeed layered and ever-folded into themselves, is that much like the pages of a book, they offer renewable, redeeming energy every time you choose to re-read the story. No different than big, heavy, timeless books that carry the beautiful yet burdensome weight of the giants within, people are also beautiful and burdensome.

With books, like with our relationships, in one moment there is blissful mystery and magic in cracking open the breast and diving head-first into the deliciousness of a new story. Yet, there is still the disappointment, the frustration, and the fear as we traverse deeper into this enchanting new realm. There is only something to gain in the beginning. There is everything to lose at the end. In the same way, I connect to you now, as my own heart spills over into a pool of jumbled words, strung along in a journey to reach you; I find peace and familiarity in the mirror that you are, as I choose to find my reflection in serving you a story, to impact your heart, now. I choose to reach for you in this moment in the same way I reach for inspiration, hope, and adventure; a good story does that for me.

Honoring the stories, I have found myself lost within has been my experience of what it is to heal.

Forgiveness is the antidote to the sting of relationships. Through my own journey with family, I've learned that when you invite someone deeper into your personal world, you cannot hold them to your own standards, but must rest in trusting that the standards they live by may graze you, but not scar you. Intimacy in relationships can be terrifying, but just as people are like books, relationships are pages in those books. Some are worn and tattered from being read over and over, but that doesn't necessarily render the story meaningless. It can be quite the contrary when you revisit relationships and feel into the stories of how people have helped to shape who you are and how you navigate your life. In my practice of continued healing, I take the time to revisit the stories I have woven with family, friends, and lovers. I choose to engage; to dive deeper into the stories that are mine.

From age thirteen to nineteen, I experienced my life as a world of failed expectations, confusion, and a prolonged identity crisis that resulted in the 3-month stay in a Virginia mental health hospital. After living in a hospital with schizophrenics, severely depressed and bipolar adults, and young adults with self-harm tendencies, I was released right before my twentieth birthday, to go live with my father, who I wasn't sure would be much help in my 'recovery' from depression and anxiety.

I remember leaving home for the first time. I was twenty years old and living with my mother, after being kicked out of my father's house. I had just spent 3 months in a mental hospital after both parents agreed I needed mental health support due to a threatened suicide attempt. I had been dealing with severe depression as a college student, and I had subsequently been failing all semester long due to missing class to sleep, and hide away from the world. I was under a blanket of pressure that I didn't know how to get out of, so I did what I knew how to do best as a young person: I pretended everything was fine while secretly letting things go down in flames. I was fired from my part time job at a local bank, and all of my classes were marked 'incomplete' at the local community college. While this was the beginning of a beautiful life shift, it was also the breakdown that roughed up every relationship I thought I had, and smoothed out relationships I had not truly tended to on my own before.

I had been severely depressed and suicidal for a total of six years before attempting to commit suicide by ingesting mass amounts of over-the-counter sleeping pills and drinking bleach. I was nineteen. I was emotional and highly sensitive. While many young people endure a year or two of awkward physical and emotional growth, my entire adolescence was the stress and pain-ridden incubator and catalyst for the free and fulfilling life I am living today, years later.

Consequently, I spent three months eating, sleeping, and socializing with men and women who were also forcibly hospitalized for mental health issues. Now, while my journey in the hospital as a psychiatric patient is a story on its own, here, my complicated relationship with my parents that propelled me into fierce action in writing my own new life chapters.

While my hospital stay was not as exciting as some would imagine, especially when movies and television depict mental health facilities as stark, white-roomed buildings with padding and shackles everywhere; it was an experience that certainly changed the trajectory of my life and allowed me to recognize the diversity and layering of the human experience which I had been completely sheltered from prior to being a patient myself. I met many men and women who related to me as fractals of my own parent's; who they are and how they are. Through days and weeks of group therapy, I was able to see beyond the surface of these men and women just as they were able to see beyond the surface of me. I was forced to listen and engage in their stories. I was made to participate, and not ignore the value in their pain and in their purposed efforts forward despite many mistakes and hardships.

After almost 90 days of being treated, I did feel a renewed sense of emotional strength and was armed with a new outlook on life, but I was still angry with my mother for making the choice to put me in an institution, at that time, without my knowing. I was angry because I felt embarrassed at what everyone back home was thinking and feeling about my breakdown, and my hospitalization. I was angry because I felt my parents had not done their best to relate to me and connect with me about my pain and my sadness before I reached to suicide as an option for my perceived suffering. Even though I had completed my formal treatment and no longer felt suicidal, I felt a sense of loss at recognizing I no longer had anyone else to blame for any sense of unhappiness.

Deep inside, I knew my parents had done their best to serve me as their child. They had done the best that they could, and I could not lie to myself and create more suffering for myself when I knew that every thought and feeling I was having was completely under my own control. My feelings were my own again, and that was a new energy I had to live with and navigate through as a greater part of my healing. I had suffered enough.

Time was the keeper of my memories, and after my concentrated time away from my normal life, time didn't seem to matter as much and neither did the memories.

In my own experience with identity dis-ease and dis-order, I had always felt so out of control. The feeling that there is nothing you can do to control the thoughts in your mind and rustlings in your spirit, is hard to deal with as a teen. Acceptance of how others treated me, thought of me, wanted or didn't want to be connected was overwhelming and caused so much self-defeat. The way through was to start honoring the adventure of the unknown! My time in the mental hospital forced me to surrender to a new world that I never would have imagined myself experiencing. I was stripped from the comfort of being able to hide in plain sight in my everyday life as a teenager, though something deeper and more powerful had always ruled my mind and spirit. I had only known it as depression. Now, I understand it to be determination, without a platform or a pathway up and out of my innermost self. Taking me out of the comfort of a safe life that was not serving me and thrusting me into an environment where I was forced to engage using my internal compass, awakened my soul and gave me permission to be great.

When I was released, instead of internalizing the energies of others, especially my parents, I began to engage in a storyline where I was more powerful within myself and more comfortable treading with the truth of how others showed up. Spending prolonged time with severely mentally ill, anxious, or paranoid people of all backgrounds and belief systems disarmed me from the hierarchy of my own family, and the empty embodiment of inferiority where there was truly no one to blame. I knew I could write a new story, and follow that storyline into a new space in life. This is exactly what I did.

In taking in the energy of one of my life stories, I implore you to take these words and if you choose, let this encounter be a prompt for you to begin co-creating new storylines within your relationships rather than just being a disembodied witness to your own story. Your relationships are you. Past, present, and future. Your relationships with your parents ARE the relationships with your children. Your memories with your past lovers are the fears and insecurities within your current relationship.

Ultimately, through my own great big story, I've learned that the most powerful way to live is to be fully present with the stories that have enchanted you. In doing this, you will understand them, you will accept them, and they will heal you.

ABOUT NOAH ALVAREZ

Noah Alvarez lived 20 years in Northern Virginia before moving across country to Los Angeles, California - the place he now calls home. He is a celebrated intuitive spiritual teacher and family intervention counselor with a passion for teaching communication skills (especially with parents and couples) and the mechanics of divine healing.

He is known for regularly facilitating "Meditation in the Park", throughout the year. Not only does he enjoy his work and outreach, but he enjoys a quiet intimate life with his family. He shares most of his time with his partner, Ryder, and their two dogs, Shaaka and Rocky.

BuddhaLifeCenter.org

CHAPTER 2

JUST KNOWING

Michelle Paquette

The tension mounts. Am I creating turbulence in lieu of peace? Am I confused or in denial? Twists and turns. Nothing is stagnant. Stability is a frame of mind or so it seems. It's something unattainable. I feel uncertainty overcome my entire being. My pulse vibrates, my stomach tightens, my lip quivers. The room closes in on me, I gasp for oxygen. Air. Water. Earth. Fire. Which element can be the one? Is salvation from tomorrow near? Pick a path. Any road will suffice. It's a choice. One I don't want to make. My feet are cement bricks. Movement is as stifling as the summer air…Is anyone out there?

This, in a nutshell, is life. It is filled with joy, angst and everything in between. Each moment, a decision presents itself. Which path do you take? *Sound familiar?* For many of us, this inner voice of confusion, often perplexity, screams out at all hours of the night. *But, do we choose to listen?* That is the deeper question.

That moment of choosing to listen, hit me like a bolt of lightning at 25 years old and at a quarter-life crossroads. I decided to follow my inner voice—that intuitive part of me, that sense of just knowing about what was next. I couldn't quite place my finger on what I knew, except to say that *I just knew*. As I pulled out of the driveway in my Dodge Neon packed to the brim with just enough room to see through the rearview and side mirrors, I embarked on the adventure of a lifetime. It was the start of a new chapter in my life. The road ahead on my cross-country journey was a long one, filled with uncertainty, adventure and mystery. But what I recall most about that drive west was the excitement that flowed through my veins like a child amped up on sugar on Halloween.

The moment I crossed the state line into California, I felt euphoric, almost giddy, with an overwhelming sense of peace. I felt like I was home. My soul was home. I could breathe. A sigh of relief overcame my entire being. The series of events that unfolded the next few months upon my arrival were quite serendipitous to say the least. It was at that point that *I just knew* I had made the right decision to start anew in California.

As a little girl, I experienced that feeling of "just knowing." It was the serenity I felt with my grandmother. When my Mom would tell me, "You're going to spend the weekend at Grandma's house," I was elated! I would wait the entire week, which as a seven-year-old felt like forever, but the payoff was always the same—extraordinary. I was filled with that over-the-top, little kid, type of energy, like waiting for Christmas morning, descending the stairs to see all the presents underneath the tree delivered by Santa.

Although we always took the same path to Grandma's house, the adventure always felt new and different. Since her arrival off the boat from Mirabella, Italy, when she was a teenager, Grandma never learned to drive after all the years she was in the states. She never minded taking the bus and she had the bus route schedule neatly tucked into her off-white leather purse with a gazillion compartments. What I recall most about that pocketbook was the red vine licorice which she had cut up earlier that morning with her tiny brown steak knife, breaking one long strand into four perfect pieces and then continuing on with the next vine. She had this little plastic bag, which housed all of the quarter inch pieces of licorice. It wasn't a typical baggie-type bag; it was a special one that Grandma had made from a leftover bag of pinto beans.

Knowing that I was prone to motion sickness, Grandma would instinctively pull out a piece of licorice after we paid our fare and took our seats. She would then reach into the compartment and pull out that perfectly crafted baggie. Before long, the red morsel of sweetness was in my mouth and I was content. As if by routine, we would chitchat all the way to the mall. We eventually arrived as if no time had passed. I felt no sickness from the motion of the bus. Grandma was my own personal Dramamine.

Once we arrived at our destination, we would shop and laugh and talk and then always end the day with lunch at Woolworth's. Sounds funny to say today but, back then, they had a little eatery. I have no recollection of what I ate, but Grandma always ordered a pastrami sandwich with no coleslaw, as she detested mayo and was highly allergic to dairy. I do remember the dill pickle. Grandma would cut it in half, and we would share it. I loved those kosher dill pickles (still do). Afterwards, I would get an orange Sherbet and vanilla ice cream (half Sherbet/half vanilla). It was like a creamsicle on a cone. Grandma would take a plain white napkin (the little ones you get from the silver dispensers) and position it elegantly so that it covered the bottom half of the cone. It was just a flimsy piece of a napkin, but the way she wrapped it around the base of the cone was just as beautiful as the silk scarves she draped around the base of her neck that she fastened with an adorned pin.

As I aged, there was never a time I didn't get butterflies of excitement in my stomach to go to Grandma's house. Some of her favorite things were yellow roses, hummingbirds and cooking. Everything she made tasted like a bite of heaven. She could take crumbs and literally turn them into a delicious concoction of pure bliss for the palate. She was able to turn nothing into something.

Grandma was my favorite person to be around... she was home to me, similar to how California is home to me. I felt a connection with her so deep and innate that words could not do it justice. As a writer, words always flowed so effortlessly, which is what made me realize that there are some experiences in life, which are beyond words, beyond feelings, beyond human existence. I just knew.

This feeling of "knowing" has been a common thread interwoven throughout my life. It is a theme that has presented itself on more than one occasion. I believe each one of us has a soul purpose in life, a destiny of sorts, and that purpose is for our soul to be set free to learn, to develop, and to grow. To soar high above the clouds, like a butterfly taking flight. Along this road called life, there are numerous pathways to walk, mountains to climb, hills to hike, roads to travel —and each one serves its role in our soul's development. I believe that our soul's endeavors are imprinted on us prior to our birth.

Perhaps it is because there are peaks and valleys in life and we must endure the darkness to get to the sunlight. When I found out I had suffered a severe concussion, the information didn't quite process fully with me. I didn't want to let go of the one thing I took pride in for my entire life. My intellect comprised my entire identify. For that matter, it was something that I could work at…my brain was an area of life that I took for granted. It was "just there."

My tenacity, personality, creativity, humor, ability to communicate and write —that all was comprised of my different parts of my left/right brain. With my brain damaged, I was at a loss about who I was and who I was to become. This life-changing experience made me fascinated with the psychology of the brain and its function and who I was as a person and beyond that, as a soul. This pivotal moment in life set the stage for a deep analysis into self and a connection within.

Even with all of the frustration of waiting and the angst of being left without answers, I felt an unbelievable sense of inner peace and a connection to life—something inside myself that I hadn't previously experienced. It was transformational, to say the least. It was this inner knowing that overcame my entire being. And since my intellect was in a sort of holding pattern, I didn't have my cognitions to prevent me from exploring this newfound freedom. My thoughts, the negative, self-deprecating ones, were mute. For the first time in my life, I felt clarity. It was as if I could just be, in a true state of presence. I began practicing yoga during this time. I was able to feel without judgment. I was able to exist without restraints. I was able to live on life's terms.

During this time, a few experiences truly stood out to me. One being the deep desire I had to understand the brain. I saw one doctor after another. At that time, I had an HMO insurance plan, so I had to get all referrals directly from my primary doctor. This, of course, meant waiting. There's something to be said for patience, that is, except when you are in the midst of a health crisis. Then, it all goes out the window. I wanted answers! And, I wanted those answers yesterday!

Finally, after a month's wait, I saw a Neurologist who told me that I had post-concussion syndrome. He explained that the brain needed time to heal from such a traumatic event. Tasks as small as washing the dishes took me forever, I explained to him. He replied, "Even your fine motor skills will be hindered from a concussion. A concussion literally rocks your brain in the inside of your skull and since you didn't have external bruising your brain took the brunt of this fall and swelled more than usual. Truthfully, Michelle, you are lucky to be alive." *What? Lucky to be alive.* Those words echoed in my head like a broken record, over and over again. I couldn't quite process what it meant at that point in time, as my cognitive functioning was still slow. It wasn't until much later in life that I understood the severity of this brain injury and its impact on my life forever.

After leaving the doctor's office that evening, I sat outside and looked up at the night's sky. I felt ever so small and miniscule. As I embraced the constellations above me, I truly observed the grandiosity of life. The stars were magnificent. In that moment, in that snapshot of time, the beauty of living profoundly awakened me. My brain injury served as a wake-up call to me and I was ready and willing to answer the phone. *Yes, life, I am open to receiving your call and the lessons you have for me*!

Numerous life events unfolded during this time, from my relationship ending to re-evaluating my professional life. I was a Magazine Editor then, but after the injury, my ability to write and edit took far longer. It was quite frustrating and terrifying and everything in between. Writing was my livelihood and I wasn't sure what I would do if I couldn't regain this skill set and be up to the caliber I was previously. It took several years for me to get back to the level of perfectionism that I previously held myself to, but through determination and perseverance, I was able to accomplish this feat. I also learned to let go a bit of the need to be perfect. Perhaps what was even more eye opening was my newfound desire to breathe life in from a different perspective.

My fascination with the inner workings of my brain continued and I made the decision to go back to school to study psychology. The year and a half that I took to attain my Master's degree was one of my favorite times in my life. I worked full-time during the days as an Admissions and Marketing Director at a local college. During the evenings and Saturdays, I took classes. I don't know how I did it looking back, but I guess once again it was that underlying will that is me, "just knowing" that I wanted to accomplish this goal. I learned even more about myself during this time. My self-growth catapulted to a new level and I discovered the importance of introspection.

And, during my spare time, (I say with a hint of sarcasm—what spare time?) I picked up running for exercise. I lived by the beach, so it was amazing to enjoy an early morning beach run before work or classes. This also was the time I developed my love affair with the beach. The serenity I felt gliding along the sand in my running shoes as the ocean breeze overcame my entire being, hearing the sound of the waves crashing against the shore. It was truly peaceful.

Those peaceful moments in life, between all of the ups and downs, were the truest times of all. It's in those moments that all of the stress dissipates and life feels worthy of living. For, in those moments, all feels serene in the world and within. During those times of peace, holding on feels like the only way to not let them slide through one's fingers. It's in the letting go, however, in which one gains the most out of life. What I learned was that in letting go, I was able to see that which remained. Those experiences, those relationships and those changes. I learned the gift of those moments and how to enjoy them as they occurred. As time moves so quickly, it's often over in seconds.

As that small snapshot of time came to an end, another life cycle began. My beloved grandmother had a stroke. I immediately flew to Northern California to see her. I spent a week with her, talking and telling stories, as we did when I was young. Although I did most of the talking, as her cognitive faculties weren't what they once were prior to the stroke. I understood though, from what I had gone through with my own concussion. In a way, my experience prepared me to be there in a different capacity for my grandmother that perhaps few others would have been able to do.

I showered Grandma with all the love I could give during those seven days, knowing it wasn't even a quarter of what she had given me throughout my life. I just wanted her to be okay. I wanted her to be back to herself. The doctor informed me that there was a possibility that she would regain *some* of what was lost during the stroke, but she regained more than just some of herself. She made a *full* recovery! Some will say that it was just the body healing itself. I believe that although that is partly true, it was also from the gift of the love and connection she and I shared. With all of that love, the doctors were amazed by her transformation. Her primary care doctor told me, "You brought your grandmother back to life." Those words resonated with me. I found myself tearing up, as I held Grandma's hand in mine. "You are going to be okay, Grandma. You are going to be okay." Her smile lit up the room as it always did.

Life is interesting, with all of its ups and downs. We have to lean on the relationships that uplift us, like mine with my grandmother. Several years passed and although Grandma recovered from that stroke and returned home, her doctors found that she had a blockage in her leg and she needed surgery. Unfortunately, during the surgery her blood pressure skyrocketed and she had a stroke on the table. This time she wouldn't be so lucky. She would no longer be able to live on her own. My strong, independent grandmother whom everyone adored had to move into a nursing home.

I fought back the tears as I told this fragile 90-year-old woman that she had to give up her home, her place of comfort, her life. I so related to Grandma because I saw so much of my strength coming from her Italian roots. She always believed in me and I in her. I wished I could have taken her to live with me, but it just wasn't possible with the amount of care she needed.

"I'm so sorry, Grandma," I said, as I told her the news.

With a twinkle in her, Grandma clenched my hand in hers, "My dear Michelle, I will be okay."

Grandma lived in that nursing home for years and was the love of all the staff. She always had a smile on her face and an energy that words couldn't describe. And the gentlemen adored her. Would you believe she even had two marriage proposals at 93 years old? Everyone saw her light, from young to old. She was a rare soul. Her resilience and adaptability and determination were second to none.
I still speak to Grandma even now, especially when I'm going through tough times. I know she is listening, even though I can no longer pick up the phone and call her or

see her beautiful face or hear her infectious laugh. I know her spirit lives on in me. For that, I am so immensely filled with gratitude.

One of my biggest regrets in life is that I never had a child of my own for Grandma to meet. I always had this strong desire for my baby to know my grandmother. When I was going through some health problems recently, I pulled my strength from her. Funny thing about being healthy is it's something you take for granted.

At the age of 42, my miscarriage served as a devastating reminder that I may never be a mother. To lose a life, one in which you could feel growing and developing, is like no other loss in life. It is a death and there is grief. What separates losing your unborn child from the death of a loved one is that you are grieving the loss of a child you only knew from within yourself.

It is a connection that I felt in my body. It is the loss of a dream that I would never experience. It is a life that I would never know, but a love that I would never forget. I felt the most intense betrayal by my own body that I have ever experienced. I was angry, but I couldn't escape the person I was angry with the most…myself.

As a woman, words are inexplicable to share what that does to your soul. For me, I have had to spend a lot of time grieving not only the loss of my unborn child but also mourning the possibility of what could have been and what might never be.

"Mommy, I Love You" … those three little words, I will never hear. Those two little eyes, I will never see. Those 10 little fingers and toes, I will never touch.
It has taken me a lot of time, endless tears, countless

sleepless nights and 20 additional pounds to finally process the most devastating day in my life. To say I grieved was an understatement. I went through the depths of despair and depression. There are no words to accurately describe the pain. Truly, I believe that only another person who has gone through the loss of a miscarriage, a life inside, will ever know the pain.

The words that changed my life came from a doctor, **"There. Is. No. Heartbeat."**

That day, I went to the doctor's office for a routine checkup and to hear the heartbeat. I sat there looking at the monitor, with this perfect baby, whose heartbeat I saw just a month before and today there was no heartbeat. Instead of the fast-paced sound of the heart rate, the room went silent. The doctor, I intuitively sensed, didn't have the words. What words are the right words to tell a woman who so desperately wanted a child that those hopes are shattered? **There. Are. No. Words.**

I had many people tell me, "Just get back to living your life." That's perhaps the hardest thing to do. I lost a life and in that process of losing this life, a part of me also died. With my "death," came the death of my hopes, dreams and promises. The hopes of being a mother; the dreams of my child's first words; the promises of my body to do as nature does; the delight of giving my parents a grandchild. All. Those. Hopes. Are. Gone.

What I found even more disconcerting was the lack of people in my life that I could turn to who could understand. Although I have an amazing support system of family and friends, but even the ones who had gone through miscarriages eventually went on to have a child/children. That, by default, made me feel even more isolated. I felt like less of a woman. I felt like if I couldn't give birth, a God-given right as a woman, then my body had betrayed me.

That experience pained me to the depths of my soul. Although I didn't know this little human being, I knew of the hopes and dreams I had for my unborn child. So, not only was I mourning the loss of what I didn't know but also the loss of what would never be. It was the loss of a dream that would never come to be. It was the loss of a life that I would never come to know. It was the loss of a role I would never be able to experience.

Acceptance is a later stage of the grief process. Personally, I have waivered with the ability to accept, perhaps as I have with letting go. Both acceptance and letting go are two ways of moving on from what was, what is and eventually what will be. I have found that holding on feels more comforting. That is, holding onto the memories, as that's all I'm left with now.

I felt depleted from my connection to myself. I lost touch with that just knowing part of me. Feeling so disconnected from myself, I reached out to the one person who I always felt so connected to, Grandma.

"How do I let go, Grandma?" I cried, looking up above.

No answer came to me.

"How do I move on, Grandma?"
Still, no answer.

Not only did I feel that disconnect from within but also from the one person I always felt connected to. So, I did the only thing I could do, I let go of expecting a response. In doing so, I let go of expectations. It didn't end there, though, as I felt alone. Truly alone for the first time ever. Not lonely, but alone.

Being alone is difficult, especially when faced with adversity. Oftentimes, even when we aren't truly alone, we are due to the walls we build around ourselves. I did just that…built an imaginary protective barrier and placed myself in it. Perhaps it was an unconscious coping strategy. Whatever it was, I needed to do it at that time to grieve and to protect myself. I needed to put myself first. I realized I was at the bottom of the list in my own life. I put everyone and everything ahead of myself: jobs, relationships, friendships, and family. I reflected back to the concussion and what the doctor told me, *you are lucky to be alive*. Maybe, then, it was time for me to start living. I mean, really living. "YES. It's time for me to live my own life." So, I made myself the lead role in my own life and that made all of the difference.

I believe it was because of this shift in perspective about my value in life that I was fully able to believe in myself when the medical doctors did not. I physically was so ill. For month after month, doctors were baffled. *I just knew* something was wrong. I was connected to myself enough to know that something was physically wrong. The pure exhaustion and pain I was experiencing was beyond a psychosomatic reaction, as several doctors tried to convince me. In other words, these doctors were saying that the pain was psychological and my body was reacting to the stress emotionally. So, there wasn't actually any real pain. They didn't believe me because nothing could be proven or found. For that reason, I was told that nothing was wrong.

Not being believed is difficult. If you think about it, it's tough to not have this connection to humanity. It feels extremely isolating, similar to how I felt during the loss of my pregnancy. It feels as if you are alone in this world, all alone. There's nothing as lonely as being physically incapacitated and truly realizing the vulnerability you have of facing the challenge all by yourself. For someone who has always been independent, it doesn't sound that far of a stretch; however, when you are too sick to drive to a doctor's appointment and too ill to go to the grocery store, you have to rely on the help of others—family and friends. Since I lived 3,000 miles away from my family that left friends. And although blessed with amazing friends, they themselves had their own lives, jobs and families. So, what would have just been a moment in time of being very sick turned into a pensive time of contemplation.

It's just me, I thought.

During this epiphany, I recounted how years prior I had moved out to California alone, lived by myself, gotten a job by myself. I have done everything alone so why then did going through this particular illness make life seem so frightening? Perhaps it brought me face-to-face with the possibility of the laminating one-day death. I have never feared death. I know that might sound strange, but I just haven't. I've done everything I've wanted in life, with the exception of having a child. Once again, I found myself stuck in a holding pattern. Waiting for appointments with specialists to discern what ailed me.

Finally, I found myself in the emergency room after a doctor's insistence that my appendix was the problem. The technician ran at CT scan, which clearly showed that my appendix was perfectly healthy.

"So you are saying you want to remove the appendix and see if that helps me feel better, even though it is showing up as perfectly normal on the scan?" I questioned.

Nodding her head, the Surgical Resident concurred.

My facial expression must have shown how perplexed I was about this surgical option.

"You really don't need your appendix," she stated.

Side note: after doing some research, there are different schools of thought about the "need" of the appendix. The pro-appendix school believes that the appendix does indeed have a job of filtering out bad bacteria in the body. Um, I think I'll keep it if I can.

This surgical resident went on to basically say that an appendicitis attack, although not imminent, *could* happen. I pondered to myself that I *could* also get run over by a car crossing the street today or I *could* die in a plane crash next week but I don't live my life thinking that way.

Obviously, I opted against this procedure. I was later released from the emergency room because there was no evidence of a reason to keep me. The chronic two-month pain didn't seem to be a concern because it couldn't be scientifically proven. I was sent home with a script for more pain pills and no steps closer to a resolution. Again, I trusted that inner knowing of my intuition. I continued to fight for myself and for the answers. I knew deep down in my soul that something was physically wrong and I was determined to find out what was really going on in my body.

Your body is the pathway to your soul and when it is damaged, hurt, or stressed, it will react similarly to how your car will react when the check engine light pops up. Your body needs a tune-up and you need to listen to its maintenance request. When your body sends a message it is like a red alert that something is wrong, it is time to stand up and be aware! When you're tired, you need sleep. When you're thirsty, you need water. When you're hungry, you need food. If you want to run a fine tuned Ferrari then you know you need to fuel it with the best gasoline to make it run efficiently. And so it is with the temple that is your body. You need to energize and fuel it with the best thoughts, the best feelings and the best ideas. You need to give your body permission to heal. Whether emotional, mental, physical or spiritual pain, allow yourself the gift of time to reset and place yourself on the pathway of recovery and healing.

In fact, you must trust that you know what is best for you and your body. Trust that your pain is real, even if no one else does. Simply put…listen! This pattern is the Universe's way of grabbing your soul and shaking it up a tad to get its attention. Just to be quite certain that you are listening. What if you are not listening? Well, the signs and the messages become louder and appear more frequently and become more serious.

If the pain you are experiencing is not showing up through modern technology, through all of the X-rays, MRIs, CT Scans, Ultrasounds, blood work, do not let this discount your experience. Do not let a doctor tell you it is psychological or psychosomatic. If you truly know you are experiencing a physical pain, trust yourself above any professional. Be your own advocate. You will be giving yourself a precious gift to allow yourself the dignity that your pain is real and you are not distorted in your thinking.

Sadly, so many people are told that their pain is not real. Guess what? I am here to tell you that it is real. Pain is very real to those of us who have suffered chronic pain and who will fight for our rights to be seen and to be heard and to be understood. If you need to continue this fight and see as many western and eastern practitioners as possible, do it. Only you know your own mind, body, and spirit and only you know what is best for it.

Healing takes many shapes and forms. It can come from your significant other, a best friend, a family member. For me, it came from my parents. During those months when I was in such severe pain, the two people who gave me life, breathed life back into me. My Mom and Dad literally talked to me every single day for two months and listened to me through all of my tears and pain and agony. Despite all of the doctors who wouldn't believe me, I had two people who stood by my side through it all. And, isn't that what life is about?

Life is about finding your support system, those who will be there through good and bad times. It's easy to be there when times are good, but when times are bad you see the qualities of true love shine through. You know, the kind of relationship qualities you want from others. A good friend of mine told me that the one quality she looks for in relationships is reliability. I thought about it for a moment and realized how important that attribute is from a relationship. When I was so sick that I couldn't even get out of bed, I had many reliable friends who brought over dinner, took me to doctor's appointments, stopped by to spend quality time with me, showered me with loving phone calls and texts.

My life, like all lives, has been a series of experiences: from happy to sad and everything else on the spectrum. What separates me from others perhaps is just an attitude of positivity. That isn't to say that I don't have days that I'm sad, because I definitely do, but I choose to talk positively to myself and keep going. Even though we are always evolving creatures, we never truly know what lies up ahead, what is around the next bend, who we will find around the corner, when life will change. We are all human beings on a voyage. Some of us, like myself, have the desire to go deeper, to delve into the reasons why things happen. Eventually, after much perseverance, I found a doctor who discovered the source of my pain. And, guess what, it was not my appendix! After meeting with him for five minutes, he was able to figure out what was wrong.

"You are not imagining this pain and you are not making it up," he kindly told me.

Tears overcame me. Perhaps it was a sense of relief that I was right. Maybe it was the hope I received that I would get better. Most likely it was my reinforcement in my commitment to myself.

I knew that if I continued to believe in myself that I would eventually find out what was wrong with me. It was actually the Ileocecal Valve, which separates the small and large intestines and has to do with the body processing waste. What I discovered through this process of living an authentic life is that the connection I had with grandmother, with my unborn child, with the concussion with my health scare, were all miraculous opportunities to further go within. I am just another human being have a soul experience and moving through life, as I learn and evolve.

This lifelong transformation, which will continue until I take my last breath, has felt like my own metamorphosis from a caterpillar to a butterfly. In many ways, it's been a poetic blend of pain, trauma, growth, and evolution. Fear subsides as I changed into a more powerful soul, taking flight. All of my colors become apparent as to why I've struggled, as I soar high above, past the once clouded skies and burst into the clear blue heavens as a new butterfly. I earned my wings. My flight is one of new surroundings. Everything appears so clearly and mine for the taking. Through this new perspective, I see, I hear, I move. As I peeled back the past, I became a new and improved version of myself.

There are moments in life that truly shape us, and those who leave an imprint on the heart. For me, during the most difficult and challenging times, in the depths of despair, holding onto those morsels of goodness – just like that piece of licorice when I was a young girl – kept me going. Now, when I see a hummingbird or a yellow rose, I know that my guardian angel is there in spirit watching over me. I still feel those butterflies in my stomach as a smile creeps over my face because I am the lucky one. And, today, as I turn the page, a new chapter begins. *I just know.*

ABOUT MICHELLE PAQUETTE

Michelle Paquette began her writing career at the tender age of 10, winning many school accolades and awards. Since that time, her writing career has included working as a Magazine Editor and Freelance Writer, covering a multitude of genres. Her professional roles have included Script Reader and Screenwriter Coach, Marketing Director, Corporate Spokesperson, Motivational Speaker, Public Relations Guru and Media Coach. For the past decade, Michelle has worked with corporations in all areas of communications and marketing, both domestic and international, developing strategic partnerships, conducting media interviews, organizing press conferences and attending industry events and trade shows. Michelle holds a

Master's degree in Clinical Psychology and a Bachelor's degree in Communications and English.

You can follow her at the following:

Instagram
https://Instagram.com/PaquettePR

Facebook
https://Facebook.com/michellelp27

Email
mpaquette27@gmail.com

CHAPTER 3

SOME PEOPLE CALL IT POSITIVE, BUT I CALL IT MAGICK

Giana Cicchelli

When I was eight years old, I told my parents that I wanted to be a witch. My Mom looked over to my Dad, and met eyes with an equally concerned glare "Come sit down with us Giana. Let's talk." I sat with my parents as they explained that I couldn't be a witch because witches can't be Christian and don't go to heaven. With that simple explanation, I was swayed. I couldn't be a witch if I wanted to be a Christian and avoid everlasting fire. It was one of the first times my idea of what I could or could not be was answered by God.

Nine years later, in my junior year of high school, I was a devout born-again Christian. I went to church, bible study, and I was a participant in 'Club Truth', the high school Christian club. I made decisions with God on my side: I didn't do drugs or drink, and I planned to wait until marriage to have sex. When the pastor asked our congregation if we knew we were going to heaven, I always knew I was. It seemed very easy to follow these rules; I could not understand why my basketball teammates would be out fooling around with boys instead of doing homework. They told stories of beer, cigarettes and fingering. I listened with utter confusion. I didn't understand what was so interesting about boys, especially when one's school work, and thereby future, was at stake.

I found myself spending more and more time with my 'Truth' friends. The end of the school year was approaching, and it was time to elect a new president for the club. I knew exactly who to vote for: Amelia seemed to shine the brightest. She knew the bible better than most everyone, and she was even-tempered and kind; surely Amelia could lead us to righteousness. I could feel there was a consensus among the voters; she was our leader.

The next week I was unable to attend because of my basketball schedule. The following week I went to the lunchtime meeting eager to find out the results. I hadn't seen my Truth friends since the vote. A strange air was in the room as I noticed the current president, Sam, wasn't leading the discussion, sitting off in a corner. The teacher who had chaperoned the meetings stood at the front of the room. He talked about nothing that seemed important, and I looked over to my friend Eric, "Hey, who won the election?"

"Amelia."

"Yes! I knew it!" I exclaimed in a hushed whisper, "That's sooo cool, she'll be a great leader."

"Yeah, but Sam told us last week that a woman can't lead in the church, so we had to have a revote."

"What?!" I responded in the type of alienating shock that only a woman with high hopes of leadership in the church could have.

It was at that moment that I realized what the teacher was talking about. "I know many of you are angry, but Sam was acting in what he believed was God's will," the teacher droned on. His voice was monotone; the way people talk when they are tearing the seams of an emotional undertone, trying to keep control of the spillage.

Right then I walked out. As I made my way to the door where Sam was sitting, I saw the desperation in his eyes when they met mine. I showed no sympathy. I had spent my whole life speaking to God, crying to God, receiving signs from God, and suddenly I was a second-class citizen in my own religion. At that moment one foot went out the door, losing motivation for such severe loyalty to a church that thought less of me.

I heard people talking about the 'Sam incident' for the next couple of weeks, and to my amazement, the women were supportive. "Well, women can't lead a church, but it doesn't say anything in the bible about women leading a bible study."

"Well, I heard that women can't lead men at all. So we could start our own 'all women' bible study, one woman had inserted.

"No, women can lead men in bible study, just not in the church." the other would reply.

The discussion never questioned "Why can't women lead men?" Instead it was a given truth that men would not submit to a woman, and God would only speak through a man.

Imagine the song, "Losing My Religion", playing in the background when I tell you this was the same time that I started having disturbing dreams- dreams that would further challenge my understanding of God. I was a seventeen-year-old virgin losing the stability of all my beliefs, and sexual thoughts about women were infiltrating my mind.

"I am not gay!" I would scold myself. One night I was watching television, and an interview with Ellen, who had just came out of the closet, brought tears to my eyes. I yelled at myself, "Why are you crying? You have no reason to be sad. You're not gay!"

If anyone had been listening to my little emotional breakdown, they might have thought I was crazy. Half of me was appalled at the idea that I might be a lesbian, and the other half of me was pushing the subject. I had just lost my community, and now I was about to lose my God.

During the summer before my senior year of high school, I cut all my hair off, hoping to display myself with Winona-Ryder-pixie-type beauty. I still struggled with the thoughts that would sneak into my head, but it was a silent battle. The first day of high school was formal day for seniors. I bought a suit. I hated dresses, and the purple jacket fit my quirky disposition.

It might seem to the reader at this point that if I had been able to see myself in the third person, I would have had no question about my sexuality. Now, not adhering to gender norms doesn't always equal homosexuality, but in my case, it was as if every part of me was trying to tell my consciousness that I was different. But I couldn't see that. I couldn't see myself in preschool when Sarah and I would hide in the big tire on the playground and kiss when no one was looking. I couldn't see myself when I was eleven and would dress like a boy, trying to hit on my girlfriends to see if I could fool them. I couldn't see myself until Cory saw me. Cory was a breathtaking beauty with a shaved head, impeccable makeup and a stunning ability to say things that might offend others without offending others. She saw through me; past all of the boundaries that my friends were never aware of. She got right in there, into my deep dark abyss of secret desires, and whispered, "Hello." Right then I decided to let my little fantasies play out instead of practicing the abstinence vigil of thought control. I mean, no one would know what I was thinking, right? Well, God, maybe.

My internal struggle intensified. I withdrew from friends and family. I wrote depressive poems and cried in the middle of the night. I prayed to God to tell me that I wasn't going to go to hell. I had followed all of the rules. I had told people of the glory of God. I had been the perfect little Christian; I couldn't possibly lose it all because I wanted to love a woman. Months of this inner turmoil led me to ask God directly. I was done praying, and I wanted an answer. I knew God would respond, but I wasn't sure that he would approve. I couldn't take the suspense any longer. I went outside, threw my head and hands toward the sky, and asked, "God! Show me a sign."

Right then, at the exact moment the question fell off my lips, a rather large tree branch fell from the tree in my yard. It wasn't a twig, and it wasn't already going to fall. I heard the crack of the branch, and the impact of its fall as the last word left my mouth. It shocked me. Here I had gotten my sign. God was responding, but what did it mean? I looked to the sky "What does that mean!?"

It was up to me to interpret, and quite honestly I was sure it meant that I was the branch falling from the tree, only I was falling from grace. God didn't want me.

During the winter break my friend Sasi and I would go to the local bookstore, where Cory worked, at night, to look at magazines and poetry books until they closed. Cory was almost always working the night shift. I knew she was way out of my league, but I loved to imagine what our first kiss might be like. I was shy, but Sasi had struck up conversation with Cory about poetry and The Yellow Wallpaper. Over the next couple of weeks, I went to the bookstore hoping to catch a glimpse of her or maybe strike up a bit of chit chat. Mostly, I would just sit in the poetry section, hidden by lyrics and insecurity, and listen to her voice, which would echo over the tops and around the shelves, tickling my ears.

One night, Sasi and I were at the bookstore during closing. Sasi and Cory were discussing the length of time it had been since each had "gotten-some". I felt muted by my lack of knowledge. The phone rang, and Cory found out her ride wasn't coming to get her. "We can give you a ride home," Sasi quickly offered.

"Really? Great!" Cory responded with relief.

My heart began to race, and I'm sure I was blushing. "Oh my God! I'm going to go to her house," I feverishly thought. I looked to Sasi and I could tell we were both equally excited, but I could not care less about the poetry discussions.

Her apartment was decorated with Ani Difranco posters and framed frog pictures. There was a magnet on her refrigerator that said, "I'm sorry I couldn't make it to church on Sunday. I was busy practicing witchcraft and becoming a lesbian."

I was taken aback. "Witchcraft?! It must be a joke," I thought to myself. "Yeah, that's right, the conservative Christians are so paranoid about homosexuals they probably do think we're all witches. Funny."

We hung out with Cory all-night, feeling high off of the potential autonomous freedom that might be ours one day. The ultimate utopia: an apartment. In the next couple of weeks, I found myself going to Borders more often, and I would talk to my Mom about my new friend, Cory. Then the moment came, my Mom was going to go out of town for a week on business but didn't want me to stay home alone. "Why don't you invite your friend Cory over to stay with you while I'm gone? Yes, invite Cory over, I would feel much better if you were not home alone."

"Really?"

"Yes. Call her and ask."

I was amazed. I ran to the phone to call. "Cory. Hey, do you want to stay with me at my house next week. My Mom wants me to invite you so that I won't be home alone," I said in a tone just above a whisper, trying to conceal my nervous excitement.

"Really?!"

"Yeah, really! Can you believe it?"

"No, I can't believe it, and yes, I would love to stay at your house."

My insides jumped and plummeted. My face flushed. My knees shook. I could not believe that coincidentally the universe was giving me this moment in time. I mean, what were the odds that my Mom would want Cory to stay over? Why not Sasi? It seemed destined.

I sent flowers to Cory's work when the day finally came. I was so nervous I could barely eat. We rented a scary movie that night, touched hands, and traced squiggly designs on each other's arms. When the movie ended we went to my bedroom and crawled under the blankets. I had no idea what I was doing, but when she lifted my chin and traced her tongue along my lips. Some sort of primordial understanding took over, and I just followed the rhythm.

"Oh my goodness, this is why all of my friends don't want to do homework," I thought to myself. "If I had known this existed, I wouldn't be waiting until marriage either."

We held each other and continued to caress each other's skin while looking at the glow-in-the-dark stars I had on my ceiling. "Does this mean I'm gay?" I naively asked, our legs intertwined.

"Oh, Giana. You've been gay since you sat in the poetry section reading Sappho."

I giggled.

"How do you feel?" Cory asked, a sense of concern seeping in. "Is everything okay?"

She seemed worried that I might freak out about my first

42

lesbian kiss. "Yeah, I'm okay, but my fingers are tingly, and my stomach feels like a million butterflies have been let loose."

"Tingly fingers, huh? Well that's a first," she giggled back.

Falling asleep that night felt as if I had transcended the sorrow of humanity, illuminated with a new feeling of fulfillment. I was sure this couldn't really be a sin; hell couldn't possibly be following right behind, could it?

Only a short month later it became obvious that Cory and I had relationship problems. I didn't know how to make her happy, and she felt distant. A week later a mutual friend told me Cory was pregnant. Oh, the depths of hell weren't far behind.

I had told a few friends, and made abstract insinuations that I was dating a woman. When word got out at school that I was a lesbian the whispers seemed to grow like herbs, in concentric circles with a distinct aroma. My friends on the basketball team each talked to me separately, asking questions, puzzled at this new development. The star forward told me that she had heard that I was gay, but wanted to ask me directly, "I mean I didn't believe what they're saying. I told them "Not Giana! She's such a good Christian."

"Yes, I am" I said, bowing my head to hide the shame.

"I'll keep you in my prayers, Giana" she responded.

I shaved my head the day I graduated. I was done being the good little Christian girl. All my faith had only gotten me disgraced when I followed my heart.

In the years following high school, I dyed my hair purple and green. I pierced my tongue and nose. I got tattoos and started smoking cigarettes and pot. I got a job at Tower Records and moved out on my own. I dropped out of college and started reading books on alternative religions. I spent the next three years doing my best imitation of a derelict. I was in Amsterdam on 9/11, and when I returned to the States three weeks later, I re-enrolled in college. I also decided to enroll in Wicca 101 classes at the local pagan shop. If I wasn't accepted by God anymore, why not be a witch?

A traditional 'year and a day' was required to become a priestess of the Goddess. A Goddess!? My brain could barely keep the thought without laughing. For such a liberal-feminist-lesbian, I was sure having a difficult time acquainting myself with a female divinity. My first attempts at visualizing a Goddess turned out to be some bizarre mixture between Barbie and Jesus. I decided I wouldn't put any urgency into finding the Goddess and instead focused on researching different mythologies.

The classes were geared towards getting us all comfortable with practicing a spirituality that wasn't Christian. Through guided meditation and Goddess chants, we were being gently introduced to a pagan tradition, something that most of us were a bit uncomfortable with. Coincidently, I felt that the rituals did seem very similar to church, but I tried to ignore my aversion. Slowly, the realization sank in that it was not the church, or the ritual, that I didn't like but the people that I built my spiritual community with. The pagans, and the pagan traditions, were more accepting of me; choosing my path was easy.

I also started studying anthropology of magic, witchcraft, and religion to gain understanding of the origins. During these studies (both academic and personal) I found a wealth of knowledge concerning traditional healing, witch-doctors and midwifery. I began experimenting with stones and crystals in my Wicca course and discovered a personal affinity for 'energy work'. Energy work is using the natural frequency of stones and or hands to correct or heal energy patterns in an afflicted body. The Christian religion has a similar practice of 'laying on of hands'. My interest in healing was kindled.

I worked at a local diner during my initial magickal training, where I met a man who sparked the notion that I could reframe reality. I made friends with a regular, let's call him Wolf, who would sit at the counter. We originally started talking because he came in reading the Bible, and I made some smart ass comment about a new version of the Bible that was gender inclusive. I was still a bit angry at the abandonment from Christianity at the time. I thought it would propel him away from me, but it piqued his interest. From there on out, he finished reading the Bible and decided it didn't make logical sense, so he moved on to the Tao Te Ching and then some Wicca books. We discussed philosophical foundations of reality, and I looked forward to the times we had to talk. One day, I told him that I get obsessed easily, and that I don't like that about myself. He looked at me, peering over his glasses, and said, "Well, what does it mean to be obsessed?"

I responded, "It means I can't get over things. I just go round and round. I feel out of balance."

"That's one interpretation of obsessed," he responded, "but you could also reframe it as being extremely focused."

That blew my mind! From that moment on, I edited my internal dialogue from obsessed to extremely focused, which sounds like a strength, not a weakness. It was now something that is under my control, not something that has control of me. I gave myself focal points for my extreme focus, like projects or books. Now, I wasn't spiraling down in self-loathing for my inability to stop obsessing, instead I had reframed the concept and used this characteristic as a tool.

I drove to Santa Cruz the night my 'year and a day' dedication ended. I was officially a priestess of the Goddess, and I transferred to UC Santa Cruz to complete my undergraduate education. My first year of school was difficult, fighting off insecurities and the nagging whispers of failure. I had scoped out the city and found a local magick shop that had all the supplies I needed: candles, herbs and incense. Continuing to practice my spirituality in solitude, I focused most of my attention on academic achievement.

I was succeeding academically, and I had enrolled in an independent study course in my last quarter. Realizing that my schedule would open up a bit, I approached the co-owner of the magick shop and asked if she might let me apprentice. She was delighted at the idea, and I was excited to finally be interacting with the pagan community.

In my apprenticeship, I was trained in the uses of herbs and crystals for medicinal purposes. I learned that Black Cohosh would ease menstrual cramping, that a large dose of vitamin C could induce abortion, and that pennyroyal could be used for the same purpose but in large doses was poison. There was a whole world of knowledge that I had never heard of, and a whole community of people who practiced it.

I had long given up the fear of Hell. It seemed I was damned no matter what I did, but further, I was learning how to unlearn my early religions training. Had Cory told me in the very beginning that she actually was a witch, I would have never pursued her. I might have created an association between lesbianism and witchcraft, thereby in my mind proving that I was making a decision against God. This is only theoretical of course, but the timing of each experience was crucial in leading me to where I am. I often ruminate over the reality that in my mind I had already lost God due to my sexuality, so exploring further into ideas that were ungodly were permissible. I came out in the 90s when the church was still very much against homosexuality. Society has become more accepting in recent years, and for the young gays today, their sexuality may not affect their religion at all! For me, finding a life a magick was a return to my eight-year-old self, that girl who wanted to believe in all the amazing possibilities of life.

My explorations into Wicca and other religious belief systems that practiced magick whet my appetite. Magick put me in touch with power. I learned how to reacquaint myself with life but from a position where everything is malleable, and I am able to put out energy to co-create my reality. When I practiced a Christian reality, I was never in a place of power. I was always praying for God's will to be done; God was the creator of life, and I was merely acting it out. In Wicca, and later witchcraft, I was able to interact with the gods. They enjoyed my participation as much as I did! There was no predestined reality, only the reality that grew and evolved as I did! It was radical! Revolutionary reclaiming of my own spirit! I could reframe my experiences so that they benefit me, and further become a source of power. A friend of mine says that I always put things in terms of power because I have so much Scorpio in my chart. Let me explain my understanding of power: to stand in a fully embodied energetic field, seeing the shifts and tides, but strong in your own foundation. When I speak of power I don't mean taking power over others, I mean being in the flow of power. Engaging fully in reality!

Here I was, a priestess of the Goddess, and a magickal practitioner! I was learning so much new information that every day was an adventure!! During my apprenticeship, I met a local high priestess of a Stregheria coven. She liked me, and I loved the idea of learning the Italian tradition from a woman who claimed to be a hereditary Italian witch. At this point I had experienced magick, but the degree of which was pennies in the barrel compared to what was to come. In my early experiences I had read about magnificent feats of magick and assumed them to be metaphor, or a collective form of wishful thinking.

I was swept away by the high priestess, and every part of me was challenged at this time. At every turn my core virtues, feminism and anti-racism, were challenged by her. She was sneaky in her training: she knew which buttons to press and how to break a person down. I felt outside of my body, watching her manipulations take place. I knew she manipulated me, even at the time, but I was curious to see where it was going because at this point I experienced more magick, daily, than I had dared to dream existed. I watched this high priestess interact with her world in a way that was both poetic and artistic. At any moment she could shift the reality that we were both experiencing, and I would feel the shift.

Often when I talk about this experience, people will ask, "What kind of magick did you see!!?" Honestly I try to recall, but every day was such an overwhelming experience that I find it a waste of energy to explain. Further, the most amazing part, and the true takeaway from the whole experience, was a different way of looking at life. I now knew that the spirits were always around to interact. Sacred

48

places were abundant, and I could commune with the gods. I also knew magick was real, from both ends. Once, the high priestess and I were getting ready for a party, and suddenly the large canvas picture of Aphrodite above her fireplace caught fire. I knew that this woman I was with had broken many hearts before me and would break my heart just as quickly. Seemingly, the pattern she had was to seduce a young priestess, initiate them into her tradition, use their energy for a while, and then leave them. I knew when I saw that canvas caught flame, that an ex-lover was scorning her, or scorching her, as it were. She put out the flames quickly, but it was at that moment that I saw how engaging in magick was both giving and receiving.

When the time came that I felt I needed to leave, I left Santa Cruz. I knew I had to escape the actual proximity of her web, or I would get sucked back in, over and over. When I packed my things and drove back to Orange County, a fierce wind followed me home. Over the next year I was attacked magickally. I know, I know, that sounds silly. Of course she wouldn't continue to attack me after I left, obviously she would be on to her next young priestess. But I swear to you, I was under magickal attack for a full year after I left, and it was in that time that I knew I would have to up my practice to survive.

This story makes me recall Carlos Castaneda and his lessons with Don Juan Matus. Don Juan believed that no one chose the magickal lifestyle (or to be a nagual), but must be tricked to embarking on that journey:

"The tricking to which he was referring was one of the most crucial points of my apprenticeship. It had taken place years before, yet in my mind it was as vivid as if it had just happened. Through very artful manipulations don Juan had once forced me into a direct and terrifying confrontation with a woman reputed to be a sorceress. The clash resulted in a profound animosity on her part. Don Juan exploited my fear of the woman as motivation to continue with the apprenticeship, claiming that I had to learn more about sorcery in order to protect myself against her magical onslaughts. The end results of his "tricking" were so convincing that I sincerely felt I had no other recourse than to learn as much as possible if I wanted to stay alive." (A Separate Reality, Castaneda).

Like Castaneda, I had engaged with a witch, and she was angry with me. The next year I experienced dreams in the astral where my attack wounds were visible when I awoke. I saw visions of animals in my home that would retreat when I saw them, and I even had a picture portal fly off the wall! I knew that I needed to survive, and to do that I would have to dive into the depths of magick!

During this time I met my shamanic teacher. I had long romanticized the idea of apprenticing with a shaman, so when I found Esther Jenkins, I was ecstatic to learn a new magickal system of knowledge. There were many similarities between my Wicca training and my shamanic training. Both systems expected me to commune with spirits and interact with the ethereal. In my Wicca training, my altar was made up of candles, statues, and herbs. In my Shamanic training, my altar was made up of rocks and leaves. The collection of stones for my shamanic altar was an initiatory practice in itself. In finding the stones, I acknowledged the weight of my experiences, and familiarized myself with rock spirit communication. Many of the stones I collected would be called trauma stones, or stones that represented a traumatic experience I had. In the teaching I would use the trauma stone to re-inform the story, focusing on the gifts or powers I received because of the trauma.

In my shamanic training and healing experiences, I discovered that in order to step into power, I had to embrace my trauma, reclaim it, and reframe it into a gift. Now, I realize this can sound overly optimistic or cheesy, but really after a traumatic event what other option do we have? If being obsessive can be reframed into being extremely focused, then living in a household with emotional turmoil can be training for a person as a healer or a counselor. There is a saying that the shaman is a wounded healer. For the shaman to learn how to heal others, they have to be intimately aware of the process, and thus wounded themselves.

My interactions with the high priestess had showed me so much extraordinary magick, but it had also felt like a traumatic test: intimate connection with a witch that would curse me if she couldn't control me. In my shamanic training, I was put in touch with power that would lend itself to my survival. As I survived and the years went on and her visitation in dreams were less constant, I continued to have magickal experiences the took me into the depths of possibility. I am sure that I am still on a journey to new revelations of spirit, and I am excited about that adventure. I know that anything is possible, that magick happens constantly, and that I am able to interact with the spirits to create my life. This makes me feel in power; empowered.

In my life experiences, one truth has made itself abundantly clear: if you believe in something, and I mean really have authentic faith, then it is real, and the possibilities are endless. In my story and with the trying circumstances that I encountered, I always had this core knowledge that I am not a bad person. I knew that Christianity may not accept me because of my sexuality, but there was no way that you could convince me a consensual, loving relationship was sinful. When I left the church, I knew I was risking everlasting hell, but there was no way that I deserved to be punished for how I was born. When I began learning Wicca, there was part of me that was a little nervous, and then another part of me that knew I wasn't doing anything different than prayer. I was just doing prayer with props, which I expected to work. When I got involved with the high priestess, I knew when she was trying to manipulate me through insecurities, and I held tight to the truth at my core. Once I understood magick, I knew that I always had access to the power of human potential. Some people call it being positive, but I call it magick.

ABOUT GIANA CICCHELLI

Giana Cicchelli is a Sociology Professor at a handful of colleges in Southern California, an artist, author, and a professional witch & shaman. Cicchelli holds a Master's Degree from CSU Fullerton, where she studied witchcraft and shamanism from a sociological perspective. Cicchelli has been trained as a high priestess of an eclectic Wicca tradition, and as a healer in the Peruvian Q'ero shamanic tradition. She has traveled to Peru, Italy, and Costa Rica to work with shamanic practitioners, and participate in sacred ceremonies. Cicchelli's most recent book, *Magick Where You're At*, hopes to guide people, no matter their religious belief, towards a more enchanted lifestyle.

GianaCicchelli.com

CHAPTER 4

INTUITION –
CAN YOU HEAR ME NOW?

Kim O'Neill

Q: What do you call a chicken running around with its head cut off?
A: A girl who doesn't know her own power and spares herself to please others.

You know them – those people that get SO ATTACHED and OBSESSED in a relationship that they basically go crazy. They call every five seconds even though the other person didn't pick up the first ten times. They call in the middle of the night; while you're at work; lunch breaks; weekends; and don't stop until you answer. They cry incessantly and make claims of feeling on the brink of suicide. They do NOT respond well to a breakup, and they turn into someone you've **never** even seen before. You didn't know you were with THAT person! What the heck happened?!? HELP! Get me out of here. Make-this-person-*STOOOOOOOOP!*

Maybe that person has been you. I can't believe I'm telling you this, but it was once – *once* – **one time only**, no more – me.

Did I really just tell you that? ... Oh my.

The person we know ourselves to be isn't always who shows up in a crisis. While everyone else in the United States was experiencing a stock market crash in 2008, I was experiencing a crushing, suicide-inducing, meltdown from the devastating breakup of me and my best bud... Sam. Yeah, we'll call him Sam.

Four years prior, Sam and I went on a date. We had met online. It was an awesome date because we had so much fun; but I knew immediately we didn't have long-term, romantic couple potential. I wanted to be upfront with him, so I told him that. I said if he wanted to continue to be friends, that'd be awesome, but I wouldn't be surprised if he declined that offer. I was strong. I was confident in expressing what I wanted. I was okay if he didn't want the same thing.

He said "Okay." He wanted to be friends. Yeah, yeah – I know what you're thinking: That was just his way to buy more time with me so eventually he'd grow on me. And he did. About eight months later we finally decided to officially date. We attempted the being-a-couple-thing three times over the span of four years. None lasted longer than three months. Nevertheless, Sam was my bestie. We were like *this.* I was his "Boo."

He often told me he was going to marry me someday; I sometimes wondered if maybe he was right, while knowing deep down something about that just felt off. And that was part of the problem. We had become so ridiculously close – talking on the phone every night after work; getting together on weekends doing fun stuff; and sometimes just running errands. We even tried the friends-with-benefits thing; it didn't work.

The problem was that as much as I loved Sam and our special connection, I started to doubt that I also knew full-well that *he and I weren't meant to be anything more than friends.* There were so many things that were "right" about our connection, that I thought maybe I needed to force myself to like him more in that way. I thought I needed to try harder and be more open. I also kept thinking maybe he would change. He liked me so much and we had so much fun together, maybe we just needed more time; maybe in the near future he'd mature a little more; maybe eventually I'd start to just feel more attracted to him. I didn't trust what I knew I knew, and instead, I fell into a pattern of his wishful thinking.

In addition to that, I eventually realized that Sam had become my safety blanket after all the past hurts I'd endured from my absent father and failed marriage to my first love. My marriage fell apart in 2001. My father reconnected with me then died 2 weeks later in 2002. I was working two jobs (sometimes seven days a week) to barely scrape by every month and living in the ghetto where my friends didn't even feel safe parking their car outside in 2003 and 2004 (and maybe a few more years beyond that). My idea of "fun" on the weekend whittled down to buying a $5 movie from Target and a bag of peanut butter M&Ms, *if* I had the spare $10 to cover those non-essentials. Sure. It can always be much worse. For me at that time, however, it was a constant struggle trying to support myself on my own and emotionally heal from years' worth of anger, sadness and feelings of abandonment. Age 20-24 was rough for me. So by age 25 when I met Sam ... I was ready to be saved. Oh. There we go; problem number three.

1. Self-doubt
2. Using a person as a safety blanket
3. Wishing to be saved

What's that spell???? INSECURITIES!!!! WooHOO!

I had always seen myself as a strong, intelligent, independent person. I'd had prior challenges in life and gotten through those. Internally, I was emotionally strong and had a firm grasp on understanding people and how to help them. How could I possibly become so insecure? That was for weak people!

Guess what? **When you doubt what you KNOW and allow other people's desires to deduct value from your own desires, you weaken yourself – all on your own.**

In January 2008, I could tell Sam was distancing himself from me. It was unpleasant, but I guess I thought everything was still going to be okay. In other words, I thought nothing would change. January wasn't even over when he told me on the phone that he'd met someone. Mmm-Hmmmm. THAT kind of "met" someone. I shifted into panic mode. I freaked out. It was serious. He *really* met someone. I was no longer his #1. I literally felt like the rug had been pulled out from under me. Within a few days, I found myself crying heavily every day. It started out as just "Oh wow, Kim's really sad about this." Within a week or so, though, I became *that* girl. I NEEDED to talk to Sam more. I NEEDED to see him. I needed that face-to-face conversation so I could feel at least somewhat safe in all the chaos that was now swirling around me. This new development in my life – that I had zero control over – turned my world upside down. My world stayed that way for about three months.

Why did it turn my world upside down? Well, about seven months before we'd met, I'd set the intention that that year I wanted to meet a wonderful guy, who had all these wonderful qualities and that there would be the potential for us to be really good friends or something more (the "potential" – Hmmm, be careful how you word your desires; you just might get exactly that – I did!). I manifested Sam into my life. Doesn't that mean our connection was meant to be in some form for the rest of our lives? *(**SPOILER ALERT:** No. It does not).*

Okay, so my manifestation had a shelf-life. I believe my world crumbled to the intense degree it did because the root of the story didn't start with Sam. It goes back to a childhood with an absent parent; assigning meaning to what it must mean if my father was never there; adopting the belief that if you never had something to begin with, well then you obviously can't miss it; and apparently stuffing my feelings down, for … the bulk of my life (a lesson I would come to repeatedly have to learn as I got older).

I remember mailing my Dad a red "#1 Dad" baseball hat when I was about 5 years old; playing catch with him in my aunt's yard somewhere around age 9; living with him for 2 months when I was a preteen; and then being furious with him around age 16 for then neglecting my younger siblings. Somewhere in there were a handful of moments of remembering, out-of-the-blue, that I even had a Dad. I would forget he even existed. He didn't call. There were no every-other-weekend visits. I think he sent me a birthday present once, but most birthday acknowledgments were from his new wives and/or my aunt. Grateful for them trying, but I was not fooled.

At age 22, in the two-week time period we reconnected in 2002, my father finally started to have some real, meaningful conversations with me. Without outright apologizing, he essentially told me he regretted not having been there for his children. He made new promises of making sure his children weren't going to go without. He expressed care and concern for me. **For the first time, I felt as if I actually knew what it felt like to have a Dad.** It was both the most nauseating and liberating experience I'd had up to that point in my life.

Liberating, because all of a sudden it seemed as if his presence and words had magical powers. It became easier to heal from my divorce and not stress about guys in general. I felt as if I had my Dad in my corner; in my back pocket; nothing could hurt me with him on my side. Nauseating, because when you realize you accepted long ago that you didn't really have a Dad and were invincible to any feelings that void might create in you – and *then* you realize you DO have a Dad, and oh-boy – there certainly **are** feelings inside that void – it was almost too much for my physical body to handle. One Sunday, he demanded he take me grocery shopping because he felt I didn't have any food in my fridge. That day he finally said the words I had longed to hear – "I'm sorry." He died the next day.

Somewhere amongst the definitions of codependency, dismissive-attachment theory and anxious-ambivalent attachment theory is where the relationship insecurity I developed can be understood. Over time I developed the need to always be independent and self-sufficient; hesitant to commit in a relationship; but also believing that once I do commit, those I love most will never leave me. **When you get proven wrong multiple times and learn that people *can* leave whenever they want, no matter how much they once loved you, you eventually lose trust in your ability to read people and can develop chronic self-doubt.**

So, back to Sam. By the time I met him, I was tired of feeling left behind by the men in my life; I wanted something solid. Friendship or romance – I wanted something that was going to last. Even though I knew Sam and I weren't meant to be romantic, there were so many other wonderful qualities about our friendship that I never wanted to let go. Without realizing it, we both became attached to each other. Without me knowing, he detached when I wasn't looking.

I cried all the time. I couldn't sleep. I completely lost my appetite and dropped 30 pounds without exercising once. I recall getting to that point where I lost grip strength in my hands, and my thighs were weak when I walked down stairs. I had practically zero focus at work, but somehow, SOMEHOW managed to finish my final semester of college and get through my Interpersonal Communication class when we started learning about communication in intimate relationships. (Really? We have to study THIS.... *NOWWWW???* – I somehow managed. Thank goodness.)

I took 3 weeks off from work. I had to. When I wasn't at school, I was either crying, a total zombie or trying to sleep (if I could at all). Sam took some of my calls but basically refused to see me and pulled away even more. Go figure. Knowing how close we had been, that made everything hurt even more that he basically disappeared in what became one of my all-time Top 3 WORST events in my life that led to incessant suicidal thoughts. Yes. It was that bad, and it was all real for me.

My divorce was hell.

My Dad's death was deeply infuriating.

Losing my best-friend-slash-safety-blanket-slash-non-romantic-soul-mate – obliterated me.

Even though I'd had six years of private Christian school and three years of singing in my church choir under my belt, I don't think I'd ever prayed or reached out to God as much as I did during that time. My go-to phrase was "I'm not well;" because I was too embarrassed to say that I was seriously suicidal. Looking back, I can see how the intense anxiety I experienced contributed to my insomnia, which then impacted how depressed and desperate I began to feel. Or maybe it was vice-versa; research shows that insomnia, anxiety and depression are linked. As pro-mental-health as I am, I resisted seeing a therapist who I'm certain would've officially diagnosed me with depression and prescribed some type of medication. However you slice it, I was hanging on by a thread and ready to try anything at all that would lift me out of my misery. I read my Bible; listened to new angelic music I found on MySpace; learned about the healing powers of flower essences and actually tried them; and bought my first positive affirmations CD. When Sam didn't take my calls, I called friends and family and balled my eyes out for as long as they could stand. It was obvious they didn't know what to do with me, but I was grateful they at least gave me some of their time. Thankfully, one of my other close guy friends was able to come over for an hour one day and just sit with me and give me a hug. I believe all these things combined, and especially the hug, was the start to my emotionally stable comeback.

For a long time, I thought all the sadness I was experiencing was my punishment for not wanting to be with him romantically. I thought it was somehow karma. There are a lot of messages out there that tell people if you have great chemistry with someone that there shouldn't be any issues with being in a romantic relationship with them. *What more could you possibly want, and how dare you actually desire anything different than what's in front of you.*

It took me a long time to realize that the only place I ever really went wrong with Sam was allowing myself to second-guess what I knew from day one – Sam and I could be great friends, but we weren't meant to be romantic. I needed to stop trying to make the relationship be something that I already knew I didn't want with him. I had to allow myself to accept that it's okay to not be completely attracted to someone. I liked Sam a whole heck of a lot, but I was also forcing myself to like him in ways that I naturally did not. By doing that, I was only doing a disservice to both of us.

It **is** important to have love in our lives and healthy relationships with people. We aren't meant to experience life alone; and it is okay to allow others to support us, even to the point where sometimes we may rely on them. It took my devastating break up with Sam for me to finally see the deeper lesson in all this: **The most important relationship you'll EVER have in your life will always be the one you have with yourself.** From that relationship, all others are built. Clearly, I was clueless to this and didn't finally receive the memo until life screamed at me through this relationship.

At the core of who I am – is love. The same is true for you. The same is true for all people walking the earth. When we aren't connected to this greater truth of who we are, it becomes easy to doubt ourselves, have ongoing negative self-talk and to devalue our own opinions; we may get easily swayed by others and think that they have the answers that we don't. When we understand who we really are; develop self-trust; take time to forgive ourselves and others; and know that **<u>we</u> are the only ones who can make our own dreams come true without needing to be rescued by anyone**, then we'll be able to move through life more confidently and take unforeseen challenges in stride.

My intuition had spoken to me on day one. I didn't need to dig deep to know that he and I weren't right romantically. I unknowingly handed my power over to the elusive "society says" rather than accepting what I already knew was right for me. **When I didn't listen, life got louder.** Life got so loud until I was forced to hear it and see it and feel it. As strong and confident as I knew myself to be, you never know how truly unstable your foundation is until it completely dissolves beneath you and you have to rebuild something from nothing. What I learned through this process, however, is that I wasn't building from nothing. I was simply learning to see more clearly – shifting away from stereotypical worldviews and understanding that all I ever need, I already have access to.

> **"You wander from room to room hunting**
> **for the diamond necklace that is**
> **already around your neck."**
> - Rumi

As time went on, I devoted more of my energy to improving my overall wellbeing. I started to see how the cheesy, positive affirmation CD I bought was actually working. I felt calmer as I believed more positive statements and had fewer negative ones circling in my head (for the record, those CDs aren't all cheesy – just the one I happened to buy – which turned out to be a blessing in disguise, because laughter is also good medicine). My eyes had been opened to some alternative health concepts, and I delved deeper into learning about meditation, metaphysics and spirituality. I learned the importance of listening to my intuition and how those quiet, whispered messages are often the clues or links to the very things we've been asking for. **The key is to trust the process, beyond what your physical eyes can see.** I had allowed myself to believe that society's rules for my life were more valid than what felt natural to me. Had I trusted the process sooner, maybe Sam and I would still be friends today.

Then again, maybe we wouldn't. That breakup was the catalyst to me embarking on a deeper journey within myself. Rumi said, **"The wound is the place where the light enters you."** There are all sorts of traumatic life situations that become the catalyst to people around the world cracking open and getting to know themselves and life on a deeper level. As painful as that friendship breakup was, there are no victims here; it helped me find me.

Although I felt like an empty vessel in the thick of it, this gave me the opportunity to build a new foundation for my life. One where I embraced that my ultimate safety blanket is an even deeper understanding of who I am, paired with a continued connection to my higher Self. I now know with more certainty how important it is to maintain this connection, because it makes it easier for me to trust myself. As I trust myself more, I stand more firmly in my power. The more connected I am to myself, the more open and connected I can be with others – even if they want to leave.

When it comes to developing self-trust, it's okay to change your mind about something, but be sure you're changing it for yourself and not someone else. When you stand in your power, you understand that someone else's decisions don't take anything away from you, because you know who you are first. **You become your own rock-solid foundation from which everything you create next in your life springs forward.**

Whatever you are experiencing in life, no matter how massive or daunting it may seem, maybe you are on the brink of something new and amazing that you never saw coming. Over time, I learned to surrender, breathe, trust myself and ground my energy in the midst of chaos; this now helps me to move through life's messes with more fluidity. Some days I get more off kilter than others, but I now have a sturdy foundation to come back to rather than one that's just been patched up over the years after more and more unresolved hurt and anger.

I can see now that the experience of feeling like I was hanging on by a thread had a lot more to do with me not surrendering to signs and intuition a lot sooner. I kept resisting all those little whispers.

- *"Kim – He's not right for you in that way."*

- *"Kim – Go try out that church down the street that you keep thinking about."*

- *"Kim – That book you just read called 'The Secret,' its principles are going to play a big role in your healing journey."*

Not listening to our intuition is equivalent to cutting ourselves off from our Self. We're denying ourselves what we intuitively know is best for us, whether it makes sense in the present moment, on a physical level, or not … and oh, how painful that is!

We never get it all done; there will always be more life lessons to learn (if we allow ourselves to learn them). We also always have the power to embark on the journey towards our positive comeback sooner rather than later. I've learned that trying to do everything on my own often leads to me just getting really worn out, frustrated and resentful. I now practice hearing my intuition and dare myself to trust the messages I receive, as well as take action on them as soon as I can. (Every time I do, I end up getting rewarded much sooner than had I not taken action.) I've learned that there's a difference between not being considerate of others and allowing someone else's dissatisfaction with my decisions to lead me to not be considerate of myself. I've learned to be more careful with my wording; and I've learned to allow myself to not second-guess my gut feelings, even if I've adopted a belief that I perceive the rest of society believes, too. For me, this is my life – not society's.

Know that you are never truly alone. Allow yourself to discover who you really are, and when you need help, ask. Trust that help is on its way, and be open to seeing that it might come in a form you didn't expect. Then take action. You absolutely have the power to turn around any unpleasant situation in your life. It starts with asking; is sustained by trusting; flows in by listening; and builds momentum through aligned action. Allow yourself to absorb just how valuable and worthy you are, and trust that nothing can limit that except you. **Before anybody else can be there for you, make sure that you show up for yourself first.**

With love and a big hug,

Kim

ABOUT KIM O'NEILL

Kim O'Neill is a speaker, trainer, author, empowerment coach, and internet radio host. She speaks on the infinite possibilities every new day holds; how to move beyond life challenges; and how to confidently stand in your awesomeness with an open heart, limitless mind and grounded body. She often works with youth, job-seekers, and adults who struggle to understand the value of who they innately are, guiding them to rediscover and reclaim their inner truth.

Kim is both ICF certified and certified as a Law of Attraction Coach, and therefore takes a combined practical and metaphysical approach in her work. Her clients develop renewed self-confidence; increased positive self talk; the ability to see their past with fresh eyes and release old wounds; and learn how to say YES to themselves so they can experience more joy and fulfillment. This empowers them to connect with their whole self so they have a stable foundation from which to spring forward.

In 2017, Kim co-authored the first edition of *Positive Minded People: Inspiring Stories of Overcoming Adversity for Living a More Positive Life*. Kim is also a Reiki Master Practitioner, Infinite Possibilities Trainer, youth mentor, and Host of the "Every Day is a New Day" show on BBSRadio.com.

KimONeillCoaching.com

CHAPTER 5

HUSTLE DESPITE THE STRUGGLE

Bennie Mayberry

This is really a story of my mother and myself and how, through her, I learned what it means to be a survivor, an achiever, and in my own terms... a hustler.

My definition of a hustler is a person who is confident despite what they lack. And, they are able to achieve the impossible anyway. And, to me, this is what my mother did. Maybe not in the most orthodox way, and from what you'll learn later... not the most legal way. But in her way she exemplified the spirit of "making it work" that has followed me into my own career.

I was 16 years old and life for me nothing less than a prison. Home should be your oasis from the outside world. A place to revitalize and rejuvenate to be your best. As a teen, a home should be a place of love, family, acceptance, and discipline. It should be a place to process your teenage thoughts as you inch towards adulthood, a place to hone in on your identity; a place for laughs, mistakes, and forgiveness. But for me, home was my greatest source of pain — my thorn in the flesh.

I grew up in Tuskegee, Alabama. Life wasn't always hard. Before we lost everything, we lived like a typical upper middle class family. We lived in the town's best neighborhood. It was the 90's. Life was simple. Kids played outside instead of being on iPhones and social media. I was happy, inventive and a curious child, and my parents fueled that by putting me in the best schools and afterschool programs. My mother, when not pursuing her own business ventures, was a homemaker. Dinner was cooked every night, and she helped me with my homework daily. Dad was a hard-working business owner. After a long day on the job, he would pull into the driveway, and I would get the biggest smile on my face. My Dad was home! Those were happy times. My Dad had brought us up from our humble beginnings — where we didn't have a lot of money to this; a stable normal upper middle class life.

Pops went to jail when I was 11 years old because of selling drugs. After he was sent off to jail, the money simply dried up. As bad as my mama wanted to stand up and be the head of household, her own kept her from getting a job. After my father was jailed, my mother fell to drugs more and more. This took more of our money, causing us to sink into poverty deeper and deeper. So, we ended losing everything quickly. For over 3 years, things went from bad to worst. Bills piled up, and one by one and things started to disappear. We went from living in beautiful homes and having all our needs met to living in a house without lights, gas, and warm water. A day in my world was like living in a 3rd world country.

My mother's drug addiction tortured me. I hated the smell of cocaine seeping out of her door. I often found crack pipes and residue of drugs in her room. I would trash them, only to have her fight with me as she tried to find them. I couldn't go to anybody for help, because I was scared the information would get back to the state, and the state would take me away. I was scared that my mother would get in trouble with the law. And because my father was gone, my mother was all I had. So I fought for her. I fought for her life. I had to become an adult early. I empathized for my mother because she had to learn how to become both a father and a mother at one time, and she struggled to do so. For me, I lost my childhood. My innocence was gone — stolen by those drugs. Poverty was all the drugs left me and my daily routine showed it. I found it hard to see the next step - to know what to do. Going to sleep was just as hard as waking up.

Like I said, we lived in a rundown house with no electricity, no gas, and no running warm water. Every morning, I picked branches outside, set them on fire in a BBQ grill, and heated a pot of water just to wash up for school. We didn't always have soap, so that pot of warm water was the best I got many days. I went to school often with wrinkled clothes which were dirty, stained, musty, and smelly. I hated how kids talked about me at school. I agonized because I couldn't tell them what was really going on.

Food was scarce. Keeping the food fresh was even harder. We had no choice but to store food in a cheap ice chest. We couldn't keep meats past a day. Cooking had to be done before sunset on the back porch and done on charcoal or portable gas campfire grills. They weren't always efficient and rusted quickly. Every night was literally a BBQ, but not the summertime family cookout most would think. This was about survival. The taste of propane or lighter fluid marinated every single piece of meat we ate. The chemicals overpowered all flavors. So, many days I took my school lunch home with me. There was no telling if my Mom would be on a drug binge or if money would be out. I was often asked by kids why I took my lunch home and I never could tell them.

During school, I carried myself like nothing was going on. I was upbeat, charismatic, respectable, and led groups at my school. My teachers liked me and I made decent grades. But during moments that I was by myself (at lunch or in the library) my mind would cry out to God in agony. While other kids were thinking about buying Tommy Hilfiger shirts, I was just asking for the very basics in life — lights, water, and food. I wanted a mother who would not be on drugs all day and actually be a mother. I wanted a house that was not a struggle to upkeep and a place where we could thrive. At times, I felt I was dealt the short end of the stick and I had no idea the reason why.

The summers were hot and the winters were cold. Every door and window remained open during the summer to cool the house. That also meant our house was infested with bugs, bees, and roaches. I left marks on my own face where I was slapped gnats away from my ears. Some days, it was so hot we would have to sit outside. It was the middle of July, and it was cooler outside then in our house. The winter months felt the worst. It wasn't uncommon for my Mom and I to sleep in the same bed to keep warm. Often, we would sleep on the couch by the fireplace. When I tell people this, they think it was awkward for my mother to be in the same bed as a 16-year-old, but it was about survival. I would often try to sleep so close to the fireplace in the living room that the fire almost set me ablaze. I still have burn marks where ambers would burn my skin when they flew out of the fireplace but at least I had some warmth.

Living with without lights was one thing, but my mother's drug addiction is what made this unbearable. People, mostly my mother's drug buddies, came in and out of our home as if it were a crack house. The people were mostly my mother's drug pals. I would only see them when my mama was fresh with money. They were snakes and vipers. I hated them! I hated all of them! They were only around to get high with her or spend her money doing it. I viewed them as the enemy. They were helping her participate in the very thing that was destroying her and kept us bound. And besides, it was drugs that got my father into jail in the first place. And it didn't stop. My mother's addiction just got worse and worse. She eventually started selling things in the house to get money for drugs. She started with TV's and speaker systems. Then she eventually sold my trumpet, bed, and anything she could get her hands on.

At 16, I was so exhausted by her drug addiction that I eventually cried out to the state department to get her help. But in order to get her help, I had to tell them what was going on. I remember a phone conversation where I almost told them everything. I asked if there was any way to help my mama without me being taken away. They said no, and they asked me if there was anything I wanted to tell them. I couldn't do it. I just couldn't leave my mother. I hung up the phone. The most help I got were pamphlets. No matter how hard I tried, how many times I cried and begged for her to get help for herself, she wouldn't. She could not pull out of her addiction by herself. One of the worst moments for me is when I had to beg money from high school friends to pay off a drug debt she had. The drug dealers threatened to hurt both of us if the money was not paid up. I felt like I reached a new low in that moment. To have to beg for money from my 15-year-old friends to help pay her drug debts was devastating.

This was my life. It was embarrassing. I had no one to turn to. My mother was very depressed and felt powerless. I spent many nights involved trying to reassure her that she was a good mother and that money did not determine my perspective of her. She wanted to commit suicide, and I saved her numerous times from taking pills to end her life because she felt useless and a failure as a person. However, it's at "rock bottom" that something has to give; something has to change; and if nobody else changes it... who will? This is what my mother had to digest within herself. She knew no one was coming to help us and that she was going to have to do something.

For what it was worth, she was a smart women (outside the addiction) and above all she was a hustler. She may have been addicted to drugs, but to her honor, she wasn't like someone you would see strung out on the streets. There was a layer of functionality she could muster and with the functionality came some sense of smarts.

My mother created within herself a "by any means necessary" attitude as Malcolm X put it. She told me, "Bennie, we're going to do this together. We are all we got. And, somehow God will help us." Then her witty mind began to work. Somehow, she found a way to jimmy-rig the light meter to turn on the electricity in the house. it was completely illegal but it worked.

She turned the lights on only at night. She knew this might allow us to fly under the radar of the city and for a time this is how we lived; lights off during the day; lights on during the night.

Now that we had some power, she wondered how we were going to make some money. We owned a few old VCRs and figured out a way to dub VHS videos. After hours of me watching her figure it out, she made her first dubbed video from a Black History documentary. During the times when our lights were on, we used one VCR to play the Black History documentary while the other VCR recorded was playing. We could do about 8 VHS a day back to back. It was a whole operation. She would tell me, "Bennie, don't be embarrassed. You gotta make it with what you have… and that's what being a business owner is about."

She had a wonderful gift of gab and charming beautiful voice. And for her, that meant a way to make money. So every night from 5:00 to 8:00, I watched her call people right out of the phone book to sell the bootleg Black History VHS for $20. She was telemarketing. I watched her get hung up on, cussed out, verbally abused, and everything in between but she didn't give up. One by one she called hundreds of people. She went right down the list; every line in the phonebook. When people answered the phone, she would mark their name as a sell or as uninterested depending on how the phone call went. People who did not answer their phone she would put "call back" next to their name. While she would make calls, I would make the VHS recordings and print labels. I knew that bootlegging the videos were wrong, but I didn't really question because I knew we needed the money and I felt a sense of pride. I started to see a difference in my mother. She was usually sad and depressed; not knowing how to make ends meet, being a single parent, not being able to work, and feeling like a failure. But an empowered exciting person started to replace her. Every time she made a sale, she would scream in self-congratulations. It was as if with every sale she believed in herself more and more.

Eventually, we got through the entire phone book in our small town. We made hundreds of orders. We had a whole ledger book filled with past and current orders. So it was time to expand. When the power was turned on, I used my computer and dial up internet to print out white page listings of residences in other cities. She would use those lists to call and get orders for our videos. We were getting orders from cities 40 miles away and there was no stopping us. Every Saturday, my mother and I delivered the orders made that week. We called it "The Route". That meant waking up early in the morning, packaging the VHS very nice with labels, and heading out. I would use a physical map to coordinate which stops we would go on according to distance and proximity to other orders we had to fulfill. I don't know how in the world I did this with a map and at age 16, but I will be the first to tell you Uber had nothing on me. At the end of the routes, the little bit of money we made felt like everything in the world. I mean a $20 bill was precious. Food was cheaper back then, so $20 could literally feed us, provided gas, and have a few dollars extra over for a snack. Back then, you could fill up on gas for just 89 cents, a gallon so $5 dollars went a long way. It may not seem like a lot but we could make $200 to $300 a week off of this. That was a lot of money at the time when minimum wage was just $5.15 an hour in the small town of Tuskegee, Alabama. I was so proud of my Mom. I saw my mother ignite in her potential and she stirred in me an entrepreneur spirit as well. It was that true hustler spirit that showed me the way.

When the bootleg business had periodic seasons of drying up my Mom would not let that stop her. Her new-found confidence caused her to seek new products. My mother would buy items and gifts from catalog wholesale companies and sell them. We sold some of the craziest things from hats with built in mini fans during the summer to mini personal alarm devices for women. We brought in hundreds a week which was a lot for us but was still just enough for us to survive. But any kind of hope for a future it was shorted lived. After routes, the first stop we would make on the way home was to the drug dealer's house. We could not even hold onto that money for a day. One time I confronted the drug dealer and asked him, "Why do you keep selling the drugs to my Mom?" And the drug dealer had no response. I wanted to literally kill him.

On Sundays, after we ran the routes, we used a portion of the funds to go see my Dad who was in prison in Talladega, Alabama. Seeing my Dad on weekends was one of the happiest moments in my childhood. I looked forward to seeing him. For one, the prison had electricity and food. For two, prison was the only place where I felt a sense of family. The prison setup was such that we could hug and walk around and eat snacks. My Dad had a way to make everyone laugh. And, it was the one day my Mom would get all pretty just to go see him. In fact, we would both do our best to look great that day. Riding up to the prison was also special. Mom played Sade and *Jazzmasters* all the way, which all attributed to me having such an affinity to jazz music today. While at the prison, we would talk, people watch, and laugh about the past. We were big laughers. Other times, I would just watch my father's arm around my Mom and sit there in each other's presence. It was my friends' equivalent to sitting around the TV watching a movie with the family. No words were said, but everything was so loud and clear. That was one of moments my Mom remained sober and I had my Dad. We were just family and nothing else mattered.

The saddest part of seeing my Dad was that the visitation would only last a few hours and then I had to go back to my reality. I had to go home. I would again be faced with heating water with wood, cooking outside, doing homework by candlelight, fighting off drug addicts and dealers at my house, taking my school lunch home to have something to eat later, crying out to God for help, and trying to save face every time I went to school. Over that five year span, I tried to commit suicide three times and ran away from home twice. But through it all, I was able to still make relatively decent grades in high school and be a respectable model young man. I worked hard and I graduated six months early from high school. People knew me as having incredible strength, being spiritual, and charismatic.

But the worse was still to come. My mother's body could not handle the continued drug use. Eventually, she became deathly ill after a drug binge. She already had health issues on top of the drug issues and it all compounded. In the final months of her life, with the little we had, we decide to move to California to be closer to family and in hopes of better medical treatment for her. However, she died just two weeks after our arrival in California, leaving me to start my life all over again. It literally took me right back to that starting place of sixteen where my mother and I both asked, "How are we going to survive?" I was just 22 years old and only a couple of weeks fresh into California. Now it was time for me to take the example my mother showed me when bootlegging VHS and making a way for myself with nothing to my name. Hiding the tears and hiding the tears and the sadness I felt, I became aggressive about landing a career in advertising. I had a gift of gab just like Mama. I didn't have a complete college degree, I was black, gay, and felt like time was not on my side, but running those routes taught me to survive. So I took her "by any means necessary" and followed suite.

My first stop was a Latino journalism conference that I attended just days after my mother's death. Heck, I wasn't even Latino, but I knew that if I was going to get into advertising, I would have to create opportunities in the weirdest of situations. I laugh looking back, because it was as if I was the elephant in the room inside that Latino journalism conference. Despite me not being Latino, I landed a job interview with Sony. While I did not get the job, it directed me to the person who actually gave me my first job in advertising. This was all without having the necessary training or skill to even qualify. The moment I found out I got the job, I cried because I could envision my Mom make the impossible happen and I knew I could make this work.

I landed my first job, which led me to my next job and soon after, another job. Soon, I was gaining real tangible and competitive experience in advertising, which led me to start working for celebrities and corporate brands. By the time I was 28, I managed over 30 million dollars in advertising a year. This was a far cry from selling bootleg tapes on the streets with my Mom. I did not stop. I went from managing small advertising campaigns to multimillion dollar ad campaigns within three years. And witnessing of my mother's strength helped me create a 10+ year career in advertising to this day and eventually start my own very successful ad agency in Los Angeles.

At the beginning of my story, I mentioned that a hustler as a person who is confident despite of what they lack and that they achieve the impossible anyway. Just like my Mom who lacked money, a job, and good health but found a way and walked in it. My Mom did not have everything but she had an incredible power to find unique and crafty ways to provide for me when we were at our lowest. It may not have been the best way but it kept us fed and showed me just how powerful a determined mind can be and what it can achieve. I took that same energy and made a career for myself. A determined mind is a powerful character trait. Every positive-minded person has that inner hustler waiting to be ignited. It's that part of you that doesn't make you timid. It's that part of you that helps you figure it out. It teaches you how to build a house with a few bricks... or in my case... a few VHS tapes.

While the VCR is long gone and digital format has taken over CDs, cassette tape, and DVDs, I still look back with nostalgic to those VCR tapes of my childhood. And here is what I learned.

First, being a hustler is working with what you have and not being stopped by what you don't have. It's the ultimate form of creativity and repurposing. The nine short hours that electricity was on in our house, she simply did what she had to do with resources she had. To me it was 9 hours of air conditioning or heat, but to her it was life or death. The only opportunity for her to prove herself as a mother, who could provide for her child and prove she was a person who could survive.

Secondly, a hustler never complains — they create. The strongest expression of self-will is the ability to curb the need to acknowledge the struggle and before obstacles that are reality and to create solutions for a more desired outcome. It's hard. Who wants to wake up every day and live a life like we did — bootleg VHS for a living, sleeping next to fireplaces, taking school lunches home just to eat? Complaining is so easy but to what end? The weeks we made the most money, it was usually when my Mom was at her best mentally and when she was optimistic. The weeks we made the least amount of money was when her energy was low and overwhelmed by what we faced. The proof is in the numbers. Yes, we are all human, but because we are human we are powerful. That includes being powerful in emotion and powerful in thinking. The right type of thinking leads to solutions.

Lastly, the thing I learned from my experience with my mother was that hustling and following a dream may not always feel good in the process, but doing nothing can feel a lot worse. It comes down to choice. My mother cried but she didn't cry defeat. In the moments of our most need, I saw Mama keep going. She did not have time to think about how hard it was. She only pushed for something better. To her, it was like she was being chased a dog. In that moment, she didn't pause to think about how pretty the dog was, she got out of the way. Hustling doesn't mean everything is easy. Hustling means doing what you have to do so that one day it can be easy. Pushing through the pain doesn't mean ignoring the pain. It means not being victim of your pain. There are things you can only learn while in that pain so learn the lesson and move on.

Looking back at my 16-year-old self, I hurt for that boy. I long to hug that boy. But, I wouldn't do it. Because what that boy went through made me who I am today. I've frequently been asked by people what was the big "ah-ha" moment; the big climactic turn-around point that somehow took you from nothing to somewhere? In reality, there was never a big turnaround point. The situations never changed overnight. They changed by small choices here and there. I can't say that I didn't have low mental moments but I always knew somehow, I was going to be ok. I always knew that what I lacked in resources, I had in creativity, brilliance, smarts, love, and determination. So, I knew I would be ok... cuz I'm a fighter.

I tell people my story and they say I don't look like what I've been through. I say comically, "Well what the hell am I supposed to look like?" They say things like, "You could have ended up just like your Mom." or, "You could have gone down the same path as your Dad." I understand where they are coming from and that it is from a good place but I say to them that I look "this way" because of what I've gained through my experiences. What you gain and gather from adversity is ultimately the reflection you'll see in the mirror after it's all said and done. If you've learned nothing or you didn't grow in some way, your adversity is in vain.

Your will to survive is not just a matter of personality, it's a matter of choice.

What kept me pumped and going no matter what I experienced was the understanding that there is no way but up. Poverty taught me this because there was no option — no choice. Today, I treat every day like the "bottom" because it is. You can't rest on what you have done from the day before. Every moment is the bottom, and if you treat it like that, you will always push for what is above you no matter hard it is.

To those who are struggling; to those who are hurting; to those who want to give up on themselves; I understand the feeling and my heart emphases with you. You've been beaten and you've been misunderstood. You've tried to explain it to people, but you are at a loss for words. You are tired of telling the same story. You've tried many different techniques and taken many people's advice and it seems like things still don't work out for you. You may find yourself, as I did as a teenager, enabling those who cause you pain. You may feel like you never got to be a child or if you are a child that you have to be an adult too soon. I understand. All of these things are valid and are important but it's not what adversity does to you, it's what you do with adversity that makes you a success. Some of the best experiences in life have very little to do with the money you acquire. The best experiences are being with the people you love and struggle with along the way. And, it is the lessons you've learned with them that are the most important things.

I wish that my mother could see me now and see how happy and successful I am. But more importantly, I want her to know that I love her and forgive her. While her addiction made my life a living hell, I feel that it was no accident that I was to experience that growing up. I actually thank her for being a part of that narrative. Despite her shortcomings, she loved me the best she knew how and that's all I could ask for. For me, home was my greatest source of pain, my thorn in the flesh - all while being the greatest teacher I ever had. Without her, I would not have this story to tell. I can only hope that my Mom is smiling down from heaven saying, "Good job Bennie, I taught you well."

To my business partner and now my guide from the other side, thank you Mama, for being a teacher both in life and in death and may your legacy remind people to keep the hustle alive.

ABOUT BENNIE MAYBERRY

On the outside, Bennie Mayberry was an upstanding, model young person in his community and was a youth entrepreneur bound for great success. He was loved and looked up to, by his peers and community. But, behind closed doors, the challenges of family poverty, family drug abuse, molestation, and self-identity issues rocked the core of his being causing Bennie to spiral down in every area of his life. After hitting multiple rock-bottom moments, numerous starting over points, and the tragic events following the death of his mother, Bennie set out on an unforgettable journey of self-healing, self-acceptance, and a path to achieving his entrepreneurial dreams.

After years of personal development, he co-founded the successful, Los Angeles based ad agency NICH Marketing. In 2011, he founded Positive Minded People, which is one of the largest self-help meetup community groups in Los Angeles. Through his group, Bennie produces hundreds of uplifting events and content each year that shows people how to overcome their own rock-bottom moments in life through positivity and self-responsibility. He pours all of his life lessons into people so they can be their best.

By sharing his story and the stories of others, Bennie's mission is to inspire millions and to set the stage for others to share their story.

BennieMayberry.com

CHAPTER 6

DISCOVERING THE LOVE WITHIN

Jaime Aplin

Learning to love myself has been one of the most confronting, yet, liberating experiences of my life. It wasn't like I woke up one day and decided to start loving myself. It was beautifully born from me hitting rock bottom in my life and realizing that I wasn't feeling anything in my life. I was numb. I was just going through life on autopilot, feeling nothing and just existing. I might as well been a robot. And then, for the first time in a long time, I felt a little light shining within me. It was showing me that I was enough and that my life was destined for so much more than the pain that held me prisoner. The more I made time for myself, to find out what lit me up, the more I discovered who I truly was. And now feeling so truly aligned with who I am, I really do know what it's like to love me, because I do accept myself — the good, the bad and ugly. I have taken responsibility for all aspects of my life, and that has given me a beautiful sense of self, knowing that I'm the creator and the director of the story that is my life.

Not that long ago, I had absolutely no idea who that face in the mirror was. I used to believe I was a wife, a mother, a daughter, a sister, and a friend. But, is that truly the core of our being? I believe these are just titles, how we "label" ourselves, but I don't believe it's who we truly are. For me, they were just the smoke and mirrors that distracted me from really knowing who I was. Keeping me safe, yet so unbearably unhappy, lost and completely empty inside.

You see, I had experienced love. I had an amazing husband Mark who loved me unconditionally. I always felt like the most special and beautiful woman to him. We shared a loving and sacred connection from the moment we met. He was my best friend, soul mate and lover all in one. What we had was so incredibly unique. And then when I become a mum, (that is what we call a Mom in Australia) I discovered a completely different understanding of what love meant. Because when you endure all that pain to give birth and then hold your own beautiful baby in your arms for the first time, it's a love unlike anything you have experienced before. I had been blessed in my life with so much love.

I remember bringing Ella, our eldest daughter, home together for the first time. We drove home ever so slowly from the hospital with the most precious cargo we had ever had in the car. When we got home, Mark and I held each other in such a warm embrace. With tears streaming down our face, we felt like the most blessed people in the world. The fact that the love we shared had now created a little family was the most exhilarating feeling ever.

Only thirteen short months later, that we were gifted with our newest little angel, Ada. Given the closeness in age of our girls, life was busy, but I loved every minute of being a mum. I had decided to be a stay at home mum. That was what my mum did, so I thought I should do the same. Prior to having babies, though, I was a determined and goal-driven career woman, always striving for myself to reach greater places. But I decided to put that all on hold, so that I could give my kids the best opportunity to grow, feel loved and feel nurtured. I wanted my children to know that their mum was always there for them.

Once my girls both reached toddler age, the life that I once knew as a mum, slowly unraveled. I struggled to cope with day to day life and living with the burden of what I called "Mother's guilt". I didn't feel as if I was living up to the expectations of what being a mum should be like. I wanted something for me. I felt as if something was missing, but because I was a mum now, I knew that my priority had to be my children. It wasn't about me anymore. I will never forget the day that Ella was diagnosed with Cerebral Palsy. Time froze in that moment. I sat there in disbelief hearing that my daughter was going to have a life-long disability. A part of me felt so incredibly responsible for that. I carried her and gave birth to her, so it must have been because of me. I was scared for how her life would be impacted. Was she still going to be able to fulfil a 'normal' life? Because as a, mum, all I wanted was for my girls to live a happy and healthy life.

The guilt I carried was killing my self-esteem and destroying the warm, loving and fulfilling relationship I once had with my girls. I struggled to be around them all the time. I knew what my life used to feel like with them, and I longed every day for it to come back. But the more that I tried, the harder and further away it got. It was absolutely breaking my heart, tearing me apart inside. I was drowning and felt like there was no way out. My life had now become consumed with depression and anxiety. I felt as if I had no control over my life anymore, and it was nothing like I wanted it to be. I didn't feel the love anymore. In fact, I had lost feeling anything at all. Eventually I got to a point where I used drug addiction as a way to escape the life I now led.

Anybody that has suffered from drug addiction, or any addiction in fact, will know the vicious cycle that keeps you trapped for so long. You are desperate to get off the ride, but you are so caught up in it that you can't simply get off. Addiction can have a strangle hold on you that makes you feel suffocated. I had felt so numb, so emotionless for so long throughout my depression. The drugs helped me to feel. You have a temporary feeling of happiness and connection, and allow you to feel somewhat "normal". But when the drugs wear off, you come crashing down even further. And there you are again, back in the depth of the darkness, desperate to get out. Longing for those feelings to come back. All I wanted was to feel like myself again.

Battling with drug addiction makes you feel like the most "worthless" piece of shit. You know you shouldn't be doing it. You know the damage that it is having to you and those closest to you, and for that you are hating yourself even more. But, unfortunately, addiction feeds from "worthlessness". It is it's best friend. I was so far disconnected from myself, my family, and the world around me. The shame and hatred I felt for myself was so incredibly damaging, and the guilt that I was carrying was so intense that it felt like the greatest weight to bear. Then I would turn to the drugs again to make that feeling go away. I would feel happier and more connected. A time where I felt better about myself because the pain would disappear. But that feeling wouldn't last very long. Then the overwhelming negative self-talk, guilt, and sadness would flow back through me like a flooding river. The cycle continued, and as the 'lows' were harder, you needed the 'highs' even more. I was suffering in silence. Because I was still living a pretty normal day to day life, nobody knew what I was going through.

And then came my moment of truth, my point of no return. Looking back now, I had no idea how everything unfolded to get me there, but all I can say is that the Universe had a much greater plan for me than I knew at the time. There I was, sitting in a room of complete strangers, except the one beautiful lady that reached out for me to be there. We had reconnected recently since high school, and she invited me to join her. I was attending a parenting workshop, believing I had to be a better parent because of the "guilt" I was carrying. The room was packed, and I sat in the far back corner, feeling very alone. I remember looking out the window and seeing my reflection. I didn't even know who that person was. I was overwhelmed with sadness. My spirit was broken. But I had this comforting feeling that I was exactly where I needed to be. I didn't know why. It just felt right. I felt a sense of comfort in that room. Something I had not felt for a very long time.

I listened attentively to the woman speaking. She had a beautiful energy about her. You know how sometimes when you walk into a room and you just feel drawn to people. Well that was the feeling I had. I felt so much of what was spoken, not just heard. And so for the final part of the evening we were asked to write an, "I'm sorry" letter to our children.

I wrote …

"To my beautiful babies Ella & Ada,

Mummy has not been herself for quite some time and

she doesn't really know where she went. When you were both born, the feeling of pure love and devotion was there. But somewhere along the way I stopped enjoying you being there, and it just became something else on my list of things to do. It was more important to have a tidy home than it was to spend time with you. I thought I had to be a stay home mum because that was what my mum did. I took away from who I was, thinking that it was the right thing to do. I needed balance in my life, to be a mum, a wife, and Jaime, but I didn't do that because I thought by giving up it all up for you would be best.

Not everyone's journey is the same, and I should have done what felt best for me. I couldn't give you the best, when I wasn't being the best. When I finally got to the point of not coping because I was at home too much, all I did was feel guilty that I no longer enjoyed your company and resented you. If the truth be known, I resented myself for not doing what was right for me. I should have been the mum I wanted to be, not the mum I thought I had to be. I took on the belief that my mum had, and thought I had to do the same thing she did. I needed the balance, but I didn't give it to myself.

I am ashamed at the feelings of guilt and that some days I just didn't want to be a mum anymore. It was my journey to have and by doing what I thought would "please" my mum, I completely missed the mark. I do treasure and love you, and all that I have, so all I can do is make a commitment to be the best version of me, so that I can be the best mum for you. I want to empower you to live the lives you want because only that way will you truly be happy with who you are.

Your Mummy now and forever xxx"

As I wrote, the words freely flowed. I couldn't keep up with my hand. It was like every word was breaking down the walls that I had so comfortably surrounded myself with. The walls of darkness that had held me prisoner within. I had no idea at the time that I was in fact writing my truth. I hadn't known what my "real" truth had been for such a long time. It was like completely pulling down the blinds, but allowing them to spring all the way back in the same motion. There I was, standing at the front sharing my letter with tears streaming down my face. I don't know where the courage come from I could hardly speak. But there was something within me that wanted to let it out, and I did. The release was incredible. I had hit my rock bottom, been cracked wide open and brought to my knees with my head on the ground. But I had fallen forwards. I had made a commitment to myself and my girls. Going backwards was no longer an option.

I realized that night that because I didn't stay true to me, I lost my own way. I sacrificed myself because I thought it was the "right" thing to do. My intentions were pure but not true. I gave up everything of me with the best intentions for my family. I had been trying to be everything for everybody else and had nothing left for me. I had slowly diminished and became someone else. I was exhausted and overwhelmed, battling through and falling deeper into a big dark hole. I was at the point where I couldn't be anything to anyone else. I was empty. I had lost my spirit and my soul. I sacrificed it all for my family. I was withdrawn from my children and hardly coping. My marriage to my true soul mate had been lost and buried. And I had cut myself off from my family and friends. I felt very alone. I was only a shadow of the person I once was. I had been just surviving and not living for a very long time. Every day was just a matter of getting through it, and wondering 'Why am I even here?'

For me, the pain staying in that dark place was far greater than the pain of changing. I knew deep in my heart it was time for change. I had reached my point of no return, and there was no going back. The letter I wrote that night was my catalyst to release so much of the guilt and unworthiness that I had been carrying for so long. It allowed the light to shine within me again, and for the first time in a long time, I felt worthy of living my life. Unlocking this "worthlessness" that I had felt for so long freed me from needing to "escape". I no longer needed my addiction to bring me the happiness and the connection I so desperately sought. I was worthy of so much more now.

For some time, I had this quote on my desk by Albert Einstein that said, "The definition of insanity is doing the same thing over and over and expecting a different result." I think subconsciously I was listening to that message every day. No more just surviving. I wanted to start living again! Time for me, Jaime Marie Aplin. Because I knew that once I found myself again... who I was, what I wanted, and what I needed... then I could have a happy and fulfilling life again. I wanted to be the best version of me. But this meant I needed to be by myself. I told Mark that I had to move out and take the time I needed for me. I needed to distance myself from a relationship we had shared for nearly sixteen years. I had been crippled by depression and anxiety for quite some time, which I knew I had to confront alone. We had tried to make it work throughout my illness, but it was a battlefield that brought so much blame, hurt and sadness. I wanted to tackle it head on, and by myself. A quote that resonated so true in my life read, "Stress, anxiety, and depression are caused when we are living to please others."

It was hard for Mark to understand that I wasn't walking out on our marriage but trying to save it. I knew that if it was meant to be, like I always believed it was, we would be together once again. I felt courageous, not scared for following my heart. I knew deep down in my heart that it would be the best thing for our girls and our marriage. But most importantly, making myself a priority was the best thing for me. I followed my heart, not my head, for the first time in a very long time. I wanted to stand on my own two feet and make decisions that I needed to for me. Without that, things just wouldn't change, and like Albert Einstein kept reminding me, I knew I had to make massive changes in order to improve my life and move forward. Yes, I was being selfish, but I stood strong by that, because being "selfless" had gotten me in to a whole world of pain and suffering. It was time to take charge and believe that I was worth it again. As soon as I made the decision to "start over", I began to feel excited for life, like I did when I was younger. It was like the world was at my feet again. What was I going to do, and where was I going? Quite liberating, after feeling like a prisoner of my own mind, a victim of my illnesses and a product of my addiction.

So, this is where my journey of self-love really began. I knew the kind of love I shared with my husband, the kind of love I felt for my children, but I had never really discovered what loving me felt like. And deep in my heart, I knew that was what my soul had been longing for. I had endured all this pain in my life to get me to this exact point, so I could truly discover what it meant to love myself. So, is this almighty quest to discover who we are, really just discovering the love within? It is the holy grail, that when we reach, we are truly saved and free of all suffering? I believe that the discovery of who we are is not a pinnacle destination we reach, but it's seeing, feeling, and accepting exactly who we are right now in this very moment. If you look within yourself right now, are you living every day to be the best person you can be, or are you living everyday seeing the best in the person you already are?

To be at our true sense of self, is to be that of love — the love for which we were unconditionally born with. It is nothing external to you, nothing that you have to be worthy to receive. It is your gift just for you. Love never leaves you. We just learn to tune it out when we follow what our mind tells us, not what feels right inside. Allowing myself to listen to my heart, not my head, has been pivotal in leading me to where I am today. You see, love cannot be created by our mind. Love can only be felt. Any emotion that is not derived from love, comes from fear. And fear is created in the mind. They are "thought" into creation, not felt into creation. You don't just feel doubt and then think about it. You think, then it projects into your reality and then you feel it. You are love, and love is you. Accepting all of who you are, who you have been, and who you always will be. For no matter where you are in your life, accept all of you and know you are only doing the very best you can with what you know at any moment in your life. And that is more than enough.

So, when I stated earlier that learning to love myself was both confronting and liberating, it's because every day that I accept more of the shadows that exist within me, it brings me to the light of my true self. I am seeing life through loving eyes. Because the more I trust that everything is just divinely perfect for me, the more I know how truly complete I already am. And, even when things get tough, the challenges are there to teach us — to help us to grow. It's even more reason to love yourself. And whilst I live in this lifetime and am learning to accept all that I am, have been, and will be, I feel the divine feeling of unconditional love. Because it's not a destination you strive to get to, it can be held in each moment we are blessed with every day. Loving yourself through it all, no matter where you're at. You have the power in loving all of you, right here and right now. But it must begin with you.

The moment that I decided to "own my story" — the good, the bad, and the ugly, I started to set myself free. Because everything that I had done in my life had gotten me to that moment, and I was grateful. Grateful for the gifts that I had received, even though at the time, they felt like the greatest weights to bear. It wasn't my past that had changed, but it was the perspective and my willingness to love myself through it that had changed. I opened up my heart to loving me, and I will be forever blessed that I decided that I was worth love.

For me now, *that* love has created a life that I never thought possible. This is the first time I have felt truly connected, happy, or fulfilled in my life. All of the pain has been worth every minute to be where I am today. For now, I live a life of purpose, not just existence. I know there is a much greater meaning to what I have been through and how I can gift that to others. I feel so aligned with who I am and why I am here. Our family has never been so filled with joy and love. We spend a lot of time together and really being present in the moment of what we have. The relationship that I have now with my girls is so incredibly special. They are my greatest teachers, as they help me to strengthen the love I have for myself and for them. In following my heart and my dreams, I know that I am being the best role model to them so they can follow their heart too. For Mark and I, our bond has never been stronger. We are both following our hearts and what fills us up, and so together we have a deeper love than ever before, and that only continues to grow. Some days it's hard to comprehend that this is our life now because it is so different to the life we once used to live. It's a true blessing, and one that I never take for granted.

We are all worthy of love. That is why we are here. My heart knows it, and so does yours. Just allow yourself to feel it too. Because when you open your heart to love, it will come flooding through like a river running back down a stream that it once created. Your heart always remembers. And when you truly feel it, you will know. Love is eternally waiting to be received.

ABOUT JAIME APLIN

I am a speaker, retreat facilitator, author and transformational mentor. I create space to help others uncover the love they have within themselves and allow them to feel "FREE TO BE ME".

Much of my own personal journey has been to discover my own SELF LOVE. A love that I had never truly experienced before.

Learning to love myself has been one of the most confronting, yet liberating experiences of my life. It wasn't like I just woke up one day and decided to start loving myself, it was beautifully born from me hitting rock bottom in my life, and living my darkest hour. I was struggling in the depths of depression, living a life paralyzed with anxiety, and trying to escape the reality of the world as I knew it. I wasn't feeling anything in my life, I was numb. And then, for the first time in a long time, I felt a little light shining within me, it was my soul starting to awaken. It started to allow me to believe that my life was destined for so much more than the pain that was holding me prisoner.

The more I made time for myself, to find out what lit me up, the more I discovered who I truly was. And now feeling so truly aligned with my soul purpose, I really do know what it's like to love me, because I do accept myself - the good, the bad and ugly.

When we can accept our GOOD, BAD & UGLY bits, we can truly discover the love that lies within ourselves. That's unconditional love. The love that we were born with.

Because once we understand UNCONDITIONAL LOVE for ourselves, our heart starts to OPEN up to having UNCONDITIONAL LOVE for others.

That's when we can CONTRIBUTE to making the world a better place. Filled with nothing but LOVE.

One Love.

JaimeAplin.com

Facebook
https://Facebook.com/jaimeaplin

Instagram
https://Instagram.com/jaimeaplin

Skype
jaimeaps.11

Email
jaime@jaimeaplin.com

CHAPTER 7

THE TILED FLOOR

Jeremy Witcher

I said goodbye. My husband was leaving for work and I had the whole day to clean. I decided I was going to start with the kitchen. We had just moved to Los Angeles, and our apartment needed much work. So, I took to the black and white tiled floor with brush and soap.

The day prior, right up the street from where we lived, Michael Jackson had died. Helicopters flew by and news outlets rehashed old information on the radio over and over again. I listened and scrubbed – listened and scrubbed – listened and scrubbed. Back and forth, back and forth, back and forth, back and forth. Then the phone rang. My trance was broken. My husband was on the other end of the phone saying he was on his way home. Puzzled, I looked up at the clock to see it read half-past-five. I slowly put the brush down and realized I had been scrubbing the same tile all day. What felt like minutes, had been hours. The single white tile I had been scrubbing was very clean. I knew right then and there this was not ok – I needed help – serious help. How did I get here?

Understanding this question takes us on a journey back in time. A journey of good and bad, back and forth, right and wrong, black and white; and a question of who I am.

I am Jeremy, and this is part of my story.

I was raised in a Christian home; which tells you very little since there are so many different brands of Christianity – but it's a place to start. My Dad was a pastor, and my grandparents were missionaries, making me a third-generation Christian. I was a Christian because that was what you were supposed to be. It was an identity that I was born into. My culture and theology required me to accept my Christianity as an independent individual but the reality was, being a Christian was expected. To be anything less was a choice to be "bad". In the beginning, this choice was simple; be "good" and follow the rules, or be "bad" by doing something different. I wanted to be good.

My cultural and familial identity provided me access. To understand my story I need to tell you a bit about my father. My father and his father were religious royalty. Sure, it might have been a small kingdom compared to others, but when you are a big fish in a small pond, it doesn't much matter – you are still a big fish. I was that big fish. My father, as a young adult, was asked by a group of people to start a church. They wanted him to be their leader because he had already set himself apart as a risk taker when he defied the theology of a Christian university he attended. He was asked to leave this university, or as he would say, he was "kicked out". I was always proud of him for this. He knew what he believed and pursued that belief to its logical conclusion, even if it meant going against the social norms of his surroundings. I respected his bravery. My father accepted the pastorate position of the fledgling church and dedicated himself to authentically revealing spiritual truths as he saw them laid out in the Christian Bible. His reputation grew quickly, and soon people were moving from all over the United States just to go to his church. Those were good days. As I grew up, so too, did the church. I saw us expand from one facility to another, and the excitement every Sunday was palpable. People wanted to learn and wanted to grow, and this gave me a huge extended family. The church numbers quickly grew to over 500 in attendance, pushing the limits of our building. People stood in the back and watched the worship service through closed circuit TV's, which at the time was newer technology. My father needed help, and three other pastors were hired to facilitate the growth. As the church continued to grow, my father was gone more because he traveled around the globe to preach at different conferences and churches. He was always well received by his audiences, and after the services, it was typical for people to line up to shake his hand and give some tearful thanks. He was a rock star, or I should say a Christian star. Patiently, he spoke to everyone after each service. He authentically cared about people and wanted to help them.

I remember one evening my Dad was visiting one of the homes of his parishioners. It was his custom to schedule visits with each family in his church to see how they were doing and what he could do to help them. On this particular night, there was a winter storm warning. However, dedicated to his people, he ventured out in the cold, snowy night. He wanted to keep his word and visit the home he had promised to visit. As the night grew on, my mother began to worry about my father. The weather worsened and turned into a full-on blizzard. What was more, we lived an hour or so in the country. We were isolated from a lot of people. My mother finally called the home where my father was visiting. The family told her that he had left hours ago, which meant he should have been home. This was before the days of cell phones. There was no way to contact my father. Fearful something had happened to him, my mother wondered if she should call the police. We waited and waited well into the night until the door fumbled open and in stumbled my father wet and cold with icicles hanging from his hair. His face was frozen, and he could barely move. The family car had broken down, and he had walked home some ten-plus miles in the blizzard wearing his dress shoes and suit — hardly attire fit for trekking over ice-covered roads. This was an example of how committed my father was to his church and the people in that church. He loved them and wanted the best for them, even if it meant he was uncomfortable or had to sacrifice something of himself. I admired that about him. However, his dedication to his work was not without consequence. He started to be drained and tired all the time. Doctors said he was anemic and had low blood sugar. The fact was, he was not being spiritually rejuvenated. But for me, life continued to be good. Everywhere I went I was loved and accepted for who my father was. I started to travel with my father all over the world and saw more before I was a teen than most people see their entire lifetime.

In my early youth, I was a strange, dark little boy – at least that is how I felt. I loved nature and animals. I particularly liked horses. At one point in my childhood, we moved to a 100-acre farm. My family rented out spaces in one of our barns to locals needing a place to keep their horses. This allowed me the opportunity to get a horse myself. That horse barn was breathtaking. It was old and creepy and full of stories and secrets that were perfect for any child. I loved working in the horse barn. It was magic to me. The smell, the hay, and the dust flowing through the streams of light gave me peace. I loved every bit of it. I remember that I had to sweep the barn every few days as it would naturally collect hay and dirt on the main floor. More often than not, I used the push-broom. The bristles gave a rhythmic swoosh as I thrust the broom-head against the cold, hard, concrete floor. I listened to the repetitive motion the broom made. Brush-brush-brush. My mind wandered, and I heard voices chanting in a chorus to the brush-brush-brush of my broom. I chanted with them, and we would get louder and louder. I don't remember what I would say, but I knew I was happy. My heart soared and I felt my whole being lift. I knew instinctively that the spirits of all the souls that had called this barn home were joining in with me and my merry work. This would go on for hours until the song in my head was so loud that it broke my own trance. I would freeze. I would look around to the extremely clean barn floor and wonder what happened. I didn't know what to do. I liked the spirits singing with me, but I feared this must be wrong. Nothing of this experience matched my cultural teachings. I wouldn't dare talk about any of this to anyone because people would think I was weird. And they already thought I was a little strange. What if these spirits were bad? What if they were demons coming to take my soul? I heard about such things from the pulpit. With these fears running through my head, I would tell "them" to go away. I would scream at the top of my lungs, "GET THEE BEHIND ME SATAN!!" This was something I had heard people say in church, so I thought I would use it. And slowly the spirits went away, and the voices stopped. The fact that they stopped made me think they were bad. Maybe they were from Satan. Maybe I had been talking to Satan himself. I was sad when the spirits left, but as a young boy I thought I was doing the right thing. For the first time, I felt a split within myself. I loved the spirits, but I chose to walk away from them. I chose to be a "good" Christian.

When it came time for me to start taking on more Christian responsibilities, I was hesitant. It's not that I didn't want to be an even better Christian and continue the family legacy; I did. No, what made me pause was that I truly respected and took seriously my role in this Christian dynasty. The problem was I did not feel ready, worthy, or real. Why? I was gay; and I knew that my brand of Christianity didn't allow for me to be who I was born to be. I wanted so much to be the best Christian and put my whole self into following and practicing my religion, culture and Christian identity. But I had a nagging knowing that if I did this, I would be living a lie. This choice was harder than the first decision to turn my back on the spirits. This choice felt impossible. And believe me, I tried to make my gayness go away. I prayed hard that I would be straight. I asked God why I was being punished. Why couldn't I just be normal like everyone else? But it became harder and harder to follow God in this area. Finally, it was clear to me that I wasn't changing. I was gay. I knew I couldn't change – this was me. Now, what was I supposed to do? *God was cruel. How could he ask me to make a choice that I couldn't make? Why was he tricking me?*

I thought maybe I should tell everyone I was gay, but I was afraid of my own truth. I was unwilling to do what my father had done so many years before. He had chosen to lose one religious community to be authentic to his beliefs. It wasn't easy for him, but he did it. And the results of his authenticity created the world of religious privilege I grew up in. But for me, I was no such hero. I wanted my cushy, religious life. For the second time in my life, I was faced with a choice of which path I would travel. I decided to take both paths instead of making a clear decision. It may be obvious to you as the reader that this was not going to work, but for me at the time, I thought I could follow two directions at the same time; Be who I knew I was or be what my community wanted me to be. I really thought I could be both. So, I decided I would lie. I didn't mean to lie, and I didn't think it would hurt anyone. In fact, I told myself maybe it wasn't a lie; maybe it was just showing people what they wanted, and keeping the other things they didn't want to see a secret.

Lying became a way of life for me. If I needed to lie about who I was to keep my position, home, and community, then I decided I might as well be good at it. I became good at showing only the parts of me that matched others' expectations. But I still felt bad. Mostly because I heard that people like me were bad. So, I started believing that "bad" was just a part of me. I didn't like being bad, which meant I started not liking me. I couldn't love me, but maybe if I was good to other people, then they would give me the love I couldn't give myself. I chose to be good in public and bad in private. I created a black (equaling bad) and white (equaling good) system that I thought would work. For a while it did work, and the payoff was worth it. I had privilege, i had access and I had power. People listened to me, looked at me and loved me — at least that's what I thought. But over time it was harder and harder to switch from black to white, from the good guy to the bad guy. I felt a rip inside me. I started fragmenting. I was confused.

Then my perspective started to shift. I still wanted to be good. I wanted to be good and white, but I loved being bad and black. I hated myself for my duplicity at the same time. What was wrong with me? I knew I had to get this fixed. I knew I had to make a choice, but I kept looking at these two paths knowing I wanted them both. I remember thinking, "What if I just became really, really bad? Maybe I would become like Hitler. Or maybe I was the antichrist. I mean, someone must be the antichrist, don't they? Maybe I was supposed to be bad and I should just embrace it." This is how my mind worked. I walked around for a week as a child pondering and grieving the consequences of embracing my darkness. I felt specifically sorry for my mother and the pain I would cause her. After a week, I decided I couldn't do it. I couldn't be totally bad. I didn't want to hurt people. I didn't want to hurt my Mom. I would try harder to be good, or at least keep my good and bad in balance. But now there was a truth inside me that I had admitted to myself — that I loved both sides of me and hated both sides of me. The stress became unbearable. I fell into depression, and anyone who has dealt with depression knows what a nasty beast it can be. Still, the me I most hated — the gay me — grew stronger. There was a voice inside me that said to myself, "YOU WILL LOVE ALL OF ME!" But for now, I would ignore this voice. And since I continued to ignore my own self, my depression worsened.

I handled my depression by keeping busy. I was the oldest of six and loved the responsibility. I was, as you have already guessed, a people-pleaser. Pleasing others gave me a sense of purpose and belonging. Remember, I needed others to love me because I couldn't love myself. But as you would also guess, this didn't completely work, and the tear in my soul worsened. People could not give me enough love to fix the hurt I was causing myself. Every day I had another choice; I could either rectify the error and tell the truth (come out as gay and come out as someone who believed spirits could talk to him), or become what I said I was — a "real" Christian. Each day I decided to not decide. So, I put a little bit of myself into being a Christian (which I thought was good) and a little bit of myself into being gay and hiding my spiritual gifts (which I thought was bad).

And each day I ripped a little bit more of myself apart, and the gap between *me* and *me* widened. Again and again **I said no to my truth**. Over and over I rejected myself. Back and forth, back and forth. So, I continued a dangerous dance with my inner self; a sparing between two paths. Either way, I would win and lose. The notion that who I was at my core was evil and something to be ashamed of grew. This underlying self-loathing built a rage inside me that was almost uncontrollable. I became subject to emotional outbursts of my unregulated anger. Most people around me sluffed off my outbursts as teenage hormones, and I assumed this was a normal part of life. I had no idea the dissonance I felt inside myself was far from healthy. And through this all, there was that voice that kept saying I couldn't keep my sexuality and my spiritual connections a secret forever. And each time this voice spoke up, I would stifle it.

The years went on and took a toll on me. I was weaker and weaker. I grew lethargic and more angry. My perfect life, which once motivated me, now was my burden. I felt trapped between my two extremes. I felt trapped by the secrets I kept. So, when the time was right, I did what anyone would do; I moved away to college and tried to disappear. It had become increasingly more difficult to maintain my Christianity. But I still moved forward thinking that a change of scenery would create a fresh start. And in a lot of ways it did. My depression lifted when I went to college, and I had a new hope. There were new people who didn't know me. I was treated well and liked my new surroundings. Maybe things would work out well for me after all. The day came when I graduated from my conservative Christian university, but instead of leaving, I stayed (after a brief break) and worked as a staff member for the same university. It was like I was just asking to be caught; like I enjoyed torturing myself with my now bipolar world. The truth was that this back and forth had become my norm. This was who I was creating myself to be — a person with a bipolar sycophantic world. And I was ok with that.

Back at home, my father had moved my mother and three of my siblings who were still with them to the Dominican Republic. He was transitioning from being a pastor to being a missionary. I was surprised but thrilled that he was following his dream. For a while, he had been talking about retiring from his pastoral role. I had seen his health decline over the years but had yet to make a connection between what he was going through and what I was going through. From the outside, my father looked like he was doing everything right. I saw his fatigue as something good and even noble; a sacrifice for the cause of Christ. What I didn't know was that he was at another of his own crossroads. His lack of motivation towards the church he once loved and his desire to change locations was because he himself was changing, and the world that he had built was not changing with him. I knew things had been difficult for him these past several years, but I had no idea how difficult they had become.

My Dad would visit me in South Carolina where I worked at the university. Each time he returned from the Dominican Republic to the United States, I sensed a change in his personality. I shrugged it off as just me. After all, I was the one with secrets. I acted like a good son, and he acted like a good father. However, we were both miserable. I remember one time standing in the doorway as he was leaving from one particular visit and thinking, "Maybe I should just tell him." I stood there for a long time, just looking at him, and he just looked back at me. I felt a strong connection as if we both knew something about each other. No one spoke. Then I chickened out, said good-bye, and we went on our way. I knew what I was hiding from him, but I had no idea what he was hiding from me. The truth? I was so focused on myself that I couldn't have even seen the mirrored image reflecting to me through my father. I did, however, feel paranoid that he would see through my facade. I wondered if he knew or when he was going to find out I was gay. Even though I hadn't heard from any spiritual spirit-guide in a long time, I wanted to believe in a world that was beyond what I saw and touched. I could feel there was more. I feared that moment when I would be found out for who I truly was, and the fear permeated through every interaction I had. Living with secrets was difficult and costly.

On one of my father's visits, he announced that he was buying a house in the area. It was strange. He said it was for the family to vacation in when they came to the states. This wasn't a typical thing my father would do. My mother loved the area so he claimed he was buying it for her, but my mother had never seen the property. Anyone who knew my mother knew that she was specific about what she liked and didn't like. And since when did we have a vacation home? I would find out later that this house was to be a parting, farewell gift to our family. But again, I wasn't connecting the dots. He asked if I wanted to watch over the property while the family was abroad, and I quickly agreed. It had been a while since I had been the recipient of my family's generosity, and I took it as a sign of goodwill between us. I didn't ask questions but moved into the big sprawling house and took to fixing up what I could while renting out rooms to help pay for the property.

Then one day I got a phone call from my grandfather. He said, "I just want you to know that whatever they are saying about your Dad is not true. I believe him." The first question that popped up into my head was, "What did he do?" I didn't know anything about what was going on in the Dominican Republic. All I knew was what little my father told me on his occasional visits. My grandfather's phone call came out of the blue, and his words raised more questions than they did answers. You know how it is when someone tells you that they are a very honest person? The red flag goes up right away. Honest people don't need to say they're honest. I asked what was going on, and the story I heard read like something out of a mystery novel. I was told my father had been kidnapped and was being held against his will. If I remember correctly, he had been allowed to call the family to set up a ransom. The details were not clear, or I was not clearly listening. Everything was so foggy. Surely this was a joke. I was told the rest of my family was under surveillance, and it was thought that their phones had been tapped so all communication in and out of the family residence was shut down. Authorities were on a man hunt to find my missing father. But for now, I was to wait. My grandfather said that some of the parishioners had questioned the legitimacy of my father's claims, but my grandfather assured me that my father was to be trusted. I hung up the phone, and a numbness crept through my body. My head was swimming. The next several hours I went into auto pilot.

My Dad had been kidnapped? Allegations? Of what? How? I knew my family was not perfect, but we were good people. We were the good guys and helped people. Weren't we? Why was this happening? How was this happening? Had my father been hiding something? Was this happening because of me? Back and forth my mind raced from one side to the other. *My Dad was good; my Dad was bad. He was right; he was wrong. He was black; he was white.* I felt like I just wanted to get myself clean, and if I did, then I knew I would wake up and this would all be a dream. But I **was** awake, and this was not a dream. The truth is, I was just beginning to wake up to a fuller reality.

The next few months revealed even more intriguing and bizarre events. Three government agencies (the United States of America, the Dominican Republic, and Panama) were looking for my father. They now believed that he was not kidnapped but had tried to disappear – but why? The truth, as I heard it from others, was that my father had been involved with multiple affairs; the extent to which I am not sure. He had decided to move out of the states to make a fresh start and mend his ways. However, he started having affairs again, and instead of coming clean to his wife and family, he decided to disappear. How far he planned to take his disappearance, I do not know.

I don't remember much those days because I lived in shock. I knew I was scared. If my father had gotten caught with all his elaborate scheming, then I too was surely going to get caught. How long could I keep up my lie? The worst part was people, were looking to me as the good guy when I had been doing the very thing my Dad had been doing – lying! Now, to keep up my Christian persona, I had to be the judge over my Dad. What right did I have to do that? I knew why my father wanted to disappear. After all, wasn't that what I had done? I disappeared to college. Now I knew why he went to the Dominican Republic. It was not to be a missionary; it was to run from who he was. I got that. I knew what it was like to want to disappear and make it all go away. I knew the price of running from one's own truth. But one nagging question I had was why my father ever stopped being his true self. In the beginning, he had chosen quickly and firmly to follow his truth by choosing his theological beliefs over that of his alma mater. That wasn't easy. He had lost a lot; but then he also gained a lot. What had changed? Why had he gotten stuck between two choices like I had? I had a sympathy for my father because I knew exactly what he was going through. The only difference between him and me was that he got caught and

I didn't. I was bad too. I was gay and hiding my desire to talk to "demon" spirits. He was bad. He was an adulterer. He was good. He was a pastor, mentor and healer of souls. I was good because I wanted to help and love people. He was good and bad; I was good and bad. We were both dark and light. We both had chosen to live in these two worlds and now these worlds were crumbling. Would I give up and allow them to crumble? No, I would fix this.

The news came that my father had been found. It brought no relief to my soul. I dreaded seeing him; the future version of me. I drove up from South Carolina to Michigan to meet my father at the airport where he had been flown in from the Dominican Republic. I will never forget seeing my father step off that plane. He was an emaciated man. He barely moved as he shuffled down the airport corridor. He looked like he had been through a war. Was this who I was to become? I took him back to South Carolina along with my grandmother and grandfather and tried to make everyone as comfortable as possible in the new family home. My father didn't talk much or eat much. He was in a severe state of shock and depression. I don't know if I just didn't want to know or if I still didn't believe what was going on, but I never asked him any questions. I just watched. Time seemed to stand still.

I remember looking out the kitchen window as my father stood in the backyard. My Dad had asked to help around the house, and I said that the leaves in the yard needed to be raked. He raked leaves from one side of a small patch of ground to the other and then back again. He did this for hours, making no progress. Back and forth, back and forth, back and forth he raked. Each time I checked on him he was in the same patch of the yard. He didn't seem to realize what he was doing. He just kept swinging the rake back and forth, back and forth, back and forth. It was hypnotic to watch him. I didn't know what to do or where to begin. How was I going to fix this? As soon as I had asked that question, I knew the answer. I couldn't fix him. I wasn't supposed to fix him. I was supposed to fix me. I knew if I kept up my secrets I too would be exactly where my father was.

I sat with my father for days listening to the phone calls that came in from all over the world. Some people called to say they still loved my father, but others called to spew their hate for him and what he had done. I didn't know what to think. I agreed with everything. I loved him and disliked him at the same time. The irony was rich because I loved me and hated me at the same time, too. My family was angry my father had lied about being held hostage. I thought differently. He was a hostage — that was true — only he wasn't being held by other people. He had held himself hostage by his own choices, and of course, so had I.

I remember one powerful conversation during this time. My grandmother, my grandfather, my father, and I sat in the living room one evening. I don't know how the conversation started, but I do remember that after a while my father started telling my grandfather how he felt about him. Years of pain spilled out. My grandfather had no idea my father felt the way he did, and my grandfather was hurt and devastated. My grandmother and I listened. We kept looking back and forth to each other wondering how we could fix this (I was a lot like her that way), but we both knew we couldn't fix this, and it needed to happen. The thing that struck me most was every word my father said to my grandfather could have been words I said to my father. I felt as if I was watching a replay of the same story over and over and over again – just the characters would switch. Sometimes I was the son, and then I was the father, and then I was the grandfather. Every way I looked, the reflection of good and bad, white and black, this or that showed up. I wondered how many generations this had gone on. I kept thinking, "My grandfather was his father and my father was my grandfather and I was my father." But I already knew this — I WAS MY FATHER. If it wasn't clear before, it sure was clear now. I was him, and I was getting to see what was going to happen to me if I continued keeping secrets and ripping myself apart. I didn't know how I was going to do it, but after watching this conversation I determined one thing; I was going to break this cycle. I was going to be truthful with myself and others. I was going to heal myself. Now more than ever, this was my chance to do something positive for my family. I was going to step up and be (possibly for the first time) the real deal. I was going to make a choice. I was going to come out as… a full-blown Christian. I was going to be the best Christian ever. I would love and forgive and put us back together. I was still hurting, but I wasn't the only one hurting. My family was also in great distress, so I made it my mission to fix everything and everyone around me. I would be a self-sacrificing Christian. I would try again not to be gay, and I would never even think of talking to anything or anyone that wasn't "real". I would **kill** that part of me. I would purify myself, and clean, and clean, and clean myself until I was pure, and white, and true, and just and righteous. Of course, that made sense. If I fixed me, then I would fix them, and then everything would be back to normal. It was at this point, I turned to the God I knew. My prayer was,

"God help me. Transform my life. Let it — the transformation — be real. Let others who knew me before not even be able to recognize me. Break open my gifts. Take my heart. Bless me indeed. Do not leave me without blessing me. God, my God, **be** my God. Show yourself to me. Fill me. Be my heart, my bones, my blood, my thoughts, my soul, my everything. Give me life."

I had no idea what I was praying at the time. I had just heard a bunch of words going up and strung them together in the best way I knew how. Oh, mind you, I thought I was really spiritual and being a great Christian with this prayer — but really? "Break open my gifts?" What did that even mean to me? Be "my bones, my blood, my thoughts?" Did I know what I was asking for? I was asking for complete transformation. Did I even know what transformation was, or did I really mean, "Please fix everything that I have screwed up?" Either way, the prayer was prayed. What was done was done.

The more time went on, the clearer it became being a "good" Christian wasn't working for me. I was very confused at this point. I had infused pain within myself; pain that I had not healed; pain that I continued to inflict. I had never gone back and looked at my core beliefs; one of which was that I was a bad person by just being born the way I was. I wasn't choosing to be a Christian as I thought. It would be more accurate to say that I was running from being gay and talking to the spirit world. Christianity, at the time, just happened to represent the opposite of being gay. So, even though I thought I had chosen the Christian path out of love for that path, I had chosen it out of fear. I was a form of godliness with no real substance. I still didn't know who I was or what I was doing. And since I still didn't know who I was or what I was doing, everything seemed to get worse. The community who had loved, revered, followed, and supported my father, of course, turned on him and rejected him. Then, by default my mother was next; and then their questioning eye turned to my siblings, myself, and anyone who had associated with our family in any way. Being a good Christian wasn't enough. The fall from grace was hard and fast. And soon it was clear my

Christianity was not going to save me. As the months went on, so did the shunning. Community divisions were wide and deep, and the reality was — we were not wanted. Now, I was nothing — turned out in the cold. Although I had personally done no wrong towards these Christians, I felt the sting of their societal rejection. I was angry, confused, and frustrated; but again, what was new? I quickly forgot my plan to reform my ways and started feeling sorry for myself. I was supposed to be good and follow the rules and everything would work out. What was the point of working so hard if it was all going to be for nothing? I started to spiral out of control. The people who I was trying to please (my family) became themselves unpleasing. I don't blame them. Each of us were trying to make sense of things and "acting out" or healing in our own way. We were splintering apart. We were ripped, torn, and broken. I remember going for long walks in the woods. I didn't know who to turn to or what to do. I wanted to be angry at my father for messing things up, but I was angry at myself. I was scared because I couldn't fix this by being a "good" Christian. And if Christianity didn't work, then my whole life had been a lie. I wasn't the only one lying — everyone was.

All I knew was that I was still gay, loved the spirit world more than ever, and my world was still in shreds. Knowing who I was terrified me the most. And even worse – I knew who I was going to become would isolate me further. *Why was I still hiding when everything was crumbling around me?* I knew the answer. Pretending to be a straight, "good" Christian was the last thread that kept me attached to a life I loved. Even if everything was falling apart, I still didn't want that life to end. I just wouldn't let go.

One day I remember looking into the mirror and I knew I had to be honest. "Jeremy," I said, "You are not a Christian." A huge release came through my entire body. I knew I was speaking the truth, and it felt good. I said, "Yes, you are right — I am not a Christian." Then I felt something I had never felt before. I felt as if someone was ripping off my skin. The pain was literal and excruciating. I thought I would pass out. I couldn't take any more pain. I am thankful today I went through this, but at the time, the shedding of my old skin was horrific. The next few days, I started to not care what people called me. The following weeks, I kept sluffing off names and ideas that I never agreed with or felt weren't mine. Since I thought God had not listened to my prayer to make me a good Christian, I would give up on him. So, I began to sleep around. I sought validation through casual, sexual hookups with strangers. Most of the hookups turned into therapy sessions where I talked and talked and talked which was probably disappointing for the other people. Sometimes I never had sex — I just talked. I could talk about anything, and these people didn't care. They didn't know me, and they didn't expect anything of me. Well, they expected sex, but I didn't care about that. Sometimes they got it, and sometimes they didn't. What I cared about was doing my own thing. I was wild and a bit dangerous, but this was the first time I was understanding me. I felt like a horse let out to pasture after the long winter months. I craved freedom and the life I had never allowed myself to have. I still felt a ripping inside, but it was a different kind of rip. It was more of a shedding — pulling off the old skin and stepping out. It hurt every time, but I started getting used to the pain. The freedom from dropping an old layer of me was tremendous and exciting, but my duplicity was far from over.

During this time I met my current husband. Our relationship was rough-going, to say the least. I would run to him and then reject him. I couldn't decide if I wanted to run away with him or run away from him. I didn't feel I could take life anymore, and at the same time, I wanted to experience more of life. More accurately, I didn't think I could take the old life I had created anymore.

While I was letting go of my old Christian identity, I didn't have anything to replace it with. I had started to reject my old self but didn't want to fully accept my new self. I was wandering around in nothingness. So, I sunk back into my depression and got worse. I had thoughts of ending it all. My anger became my constant companion, and I took it out on my husband who was the only person left in my life. By this time, I had pushed away my family and everyone from my old life. I look back on these days with sadness. I did a lot of damage to the people I loved. I have had to forgive myself over and over and to understand that I was doing the best with what I had at the time. Am I proud of this time? No. Did it need to happen? Yes. Here I started learning a reality that I know today. Destruction has a part in the transformation process; and I was indeed transforming. As difficult as destruction is to understand or accept, it is necessary.

The next part of my story I will move through quickly. The point I want you to get is that the shedding and pulling away of the old continued and gained momentum. No part of my life was untouched. Everything was being ripped away – and when I say everything, I mean everything!

My family eventually found out about me and my now husband. Their reaction was as expected. Interactions were incredibly tense, and still no one talked about it. The fighting between me and my family was heated. On the other hand, my husband was a constant rock. He recognized more in me than I could see for myself. We (or rather he) decided that it was time for a change. I went along with whatever he wanted. I trusted him as he was the first person who saw me for who I was and not what I was doing. I wanted a change but didn't feel strong enough to make the change happen for myself. I remember sitting with him on a park bleacher as he talked about God leading him to go to California. He wanted to know where God was leading me. He wanted us to be united. I played along. The truth was that I had no idea who God was let alone where he was leading me. I just knew that I had to get out and needed a fresh start. I also knew I trusted my husband and was good with whatever he decided. We decided to move from South Carolina to California.

Now that my husband and I had decided to move to California, we had to find a way to do it. Things did not look good. The 2007 recession started, and we lost our house, cars, and business. I worked two part-time jobs to keep us floating, and we moved from my house into an apartment. My husband got into a severe workplace accident which rendered him bedridden for several months. Then, I started having dreams. In one of those dreams, I saw us moving to California in a U-Haul truck. I told my husband about the dream and he said, "No, we are going to get rid of everything and take only what we can fit into the cars." I said, "Ok." We loaded up as much as we could in our two cars and set off. I just wanted to get it over with. Looking back, I can see that I was still not free from my old patterns. I thought I was making a clean break, but I was still doing exactly what I and my father had done before which was run away from problems. My life still needed to be shaken up. The destruction wasn't over. And what better sign to signify this than an earthquake.

The day before we left SC there was a 5.2 earthquake. The quake, which struck just before 4:37 a.m. local time, was centered six miles (9.6 kilometers) from West Salem, Illinois of all places and is (at the time of this writing) the largest Midwestern earthquake to date. Two aftershocks during the next three hours measured magnitude 2.6 and 2.5. The earthquake rattled skyscrapers in Chicago and homes in Cincinnati, Ohio, and was even felt as far away as Des Moines, Iowa, and Atlanta, Georgia, which happened to be the first big city we needed to drive through. As we drove through Atlanta, Georgia the next day, I saw all the broken windows on the business buildings. Everything around me was cracking and falling apart. I still didn't get the connection.

Then, my car lost power in the middle of Atlanta's rush hour. I had no control over the vehicle. I thought I was going to crash. But of course, why wouldn't my car break down? I didn't have control over my life, and I was crashing. Now I see that the universe was giving me clear and direct signs of where I was and what I was doing, but I still couldn't see it at the time. All I could see was my stupid car was going to get me killed. We pulled over to get the car fixed and then went on our way. Two more times the car started acting up, and the third time the engine caught on fire. I remember sitting on the side of the road while my car finished burning out the engine. I walked away from the car just in case it exploded; that would be my luck. I sat down and cried. I thought, "Am I doing the right thing by moving? Why is everything still falling apart? Why am I still being punished?"

I looked down on the ground and saw a ripped piece of paper and on it were the words...

"You are Loved."

I looked around and saw another paper that said,

"I know the plans I have for you."

I saw another one that said,

"plans to prosper you and not to harm you," and another paper said,

"plans to give you hope and a future."

I was sitting in the middle of all these tiny scraps of paper. A church bulletin had landed on the side of the road and been shredded by a lawn mower. I had sat in the middle of this torn up message. I collected the bits of paper and pieced them together as I sat by the side of the road. My husband was farther up the road on his cell phone calling for the appropriate help. I looked at the scripture verse that was in fact Jeremiah 29:11.

"For I know the plans I have for you, declares the LORD, plans to prosper you and not to harm you, plans to give you hope and a future."

I sat for a long time. *Was this a message for me?* "No," I said. "It's random. Some Christian idiot littered and I'm sitting in the results." But another voice said, "Can't you see? How much clearer do I have to be with you? This isn't chance. I am speaking to you. What more do you want?" "Ok," I said. "I am listening."

Needless to say, the relaxing trip we had planned ended up draining our bank account. Eventually, we had to ditch my car as it was worth more as scrap metal then it was to get it repaired. We rented a U-Haul and pulled our remaining car. The dream I had earlier came true. We continued our trip as the gas prices rose to record highs along with the heat. Once in California, we found out the apartment that we had rented was a scam, and we would be homeless in eight days. Life was getting worse and worse but for some reason it didn't matter. I kept opening the envelope I had stuffed those shredded pieces of paper in and I would take them out to look at.

A future — to prosper — I love you.

How was this going to happen? Through providential steps and hard work, we eventually secured an apartment. The catch was – it needed work.

This is how I found myself cleaning the apartment we had secured in the nick of time. Here is where my cleaning brush met the black and white checkered floor. The day before, right up the street from where we lived, Michael Jackson had died. The man in the mirror was dead. Dead! I, too, was dead or dying. A helicopter flew by. I listened and scrubbed – listened and scrubbed – listened and scrubbed. Back and forth, back and forth, back and forth, back and forth. The phone rang. I heard a voice on the other end. "I'm coming home." The clock said half-past-five. I looked at the white tile. It was very clean – very, very clean. How did I get here?

I died.

I will not say that the next few months, or even years, were easy. I would look at that black and white checkered kitchen floor and ask myself, "What do I want?" I started noticing that not all the white tiles were the same white. Not all the black tiles were the same black. Some were newer and some were faded. Some of the white tiles had the yellowing stain of age, and some were crisp and fresh. I noticed a lot about that floor over the next few weeks. But the biggest realization was that I needed both the white and the black tiles to make up my kitchen floor. The black stopped being bad, and the white stopped being good. They were just tiles, and the contrast of these two colors created a beautiful floor. They were not better than the other. They were both needed. I tried to stop thinking of my life through an either-or-perspective. I started picking up the shattered, torn, and broken pieces and put them back together. I started to rebuild. This time I would leave no part of me out. I would not call one good or the other bad. I still had black and white parts of me, but they were just that — black and white — not good, not bad. My guide was whether it was truthful to me. If I knew it to be true for me, I didn't judge it. This was the hardest shift, but through this shift, I started not being so hard on myself. Since I wasn't good or bad, then I automatically became more lovable. I found parts about me that I loved. And when I loved me, I didn't need others to fill me so much with their love. I found that if I had to let go of a person or situation, I could do it better because I wasn't them. They were not my identity. I started knowing who I am. However, rebuilding myself was not easy. There was very little I liked to do or felt like doing at the beginning. Mostly, I knew what I didn't want, which in and of itself was a place to start. But occasionally, I would feel a spark — something that caught my attention and I would go for that. I realized the prayer I had prayed all those years ago was being answered. I was being transformed. I had died and been reborn all at the same time. I was being made into the very things that I had asked for. The dualistic, judgmental, old me was gone, and in its place a new, multifaceted person was being formed. This did not happen overnight, and this work is not finished.

Today, my life has come full circle. I embrace all the religion I was raised in because I understand what it was for and why I needed it. But I understand that God is bigger than any form or system we try to lock it into. I say now, that my faith has outgrown my Christianity. Spirit and spirits talk to me now, and I understand God in a whole new way. I am surrounded by love. I can feel and hear and see things I never did before. I am still transforming, and I am okay with that. I love who I am and who I am going to be. And I love you. I love *all* of you.

ABOUT JEREMY WITCHER

Jeremy Witcher is an empathic seer who redistributes and balances energies. He currently works with his husband Prophet Calvin Witcher. Together, they teach spiritual communities through their school, curriculum, and book materials. His passion is to help those in transition; be it a transition in faith, society, or culture. Jeremy is a father of four boys, writer, group facilitator, and spiritual mentor.

JeremyWitcher.com

CHAPTER 8

WATERED, RESTED, AND FED

Drew Bensen

As soon as I was old enough, I joined the tee-ball team. I played my heart out. I was fast, intense, and all around a nice kid playing the best I could. I remember some of the Dads in the bleachers yelling to their sons, "Don't let a girl get you out! Don't let a girl beat you." It was shocking when it would happen. Yes, I was a girl, but why did it matter? It hurt then and still hurts to recall today. I wonder why I don't remember anyone sticking up for me? How come no one told them to knock it off? Maybe I just didn't hear them. I know my Dad was there. Was he embarrassed of me? Why were those Dads so scared of me being better than their sons, and for the record, I was better? Why did it matter and why were they so mean to me about it? I hid my long blonde curly hair in my baseball cap after that and tried my best to fit in. It never stopped, so I stopped playing ball until the 5th grade. I guess I learned very young to be ashamed of who I was- that I was different and not the same on the outside as I felt on the inside. Adults seemed to enjoy pointing it out to me often, noticing that I was too boyish for a "girl". Not my Dad. When I was young, he treated me like his assistant and I loved it. But that ended up not being enough. The times he needed me to be his sidekick were not enough. I was his daughter, and I was a "tomboy".

That's the universal word they give people like me. A way for people to halfway (but not really) accept you. A translation for people to navigate their brains around who someone is. Most people need to be able to look at a person (regardless if the person is an innocent child) and immediately assign them a gender. If they cannot clearly and easily assign gender or the gender doesn't match the behavior, there is confusion. That's when phrases or terms come into play.

"Tomboy! Tomboy!" I'm not sure if it saved me or stalled my progress. After all, I knew who I was on the inside. There wasn't a term or word. I was me. They (the world) were not ready for someone like me back then so Tomboy it was. All I knew was I wanted to be okay to be me not what people thought I was.

My father and I never talked about what I was or was not. We just lived our life doing fun father-"son" stuff. He taught me to ride my dirt bike and build things. We were invincible. My Mom approved in her own way by turning her bath towels into my superhero cape. She also made sure all family members knew what Star Wars or Hot Wheels toys I wanted for holidays. I had them all. In that way, my life was awesome.

All I ever wanted was for my Dad to love me, accept me

and respect me. I wanted him to treat me like he treated any male kid that came around our family. Seriously, I was jealous of any kid that was a boy. In my mind, my Dad liked them more and I felt I could never be good enough compared to them. Of course, I didn't understand what I was feeling at the time. I was just angry at these boys and would compete to do better and be better than they could ever dream of being in order to get my Dad's attention. "After all", I thought, "Why was I any different?" I thought that because I was a good person (kind, generous, funny, interesting) and because I would bust my ass doing any project my Dad needed, that he should treat me as an equal with these boys.

As a kid, I just remember doing whatever I could to be near my Dad. The night before my 6th birthday, my Dad was getting ready to go fishing. I asked if I could join. He said if I was up early enough the next day, I could go. His best buddy was there, and they both laughed because they were leaving really early and knew I wouldn't get up. But I was waiting on the couch all ready when he woke up, and that day I was the only one who caught a fish.

I loved my life when I was doing everything a son would do. I worked hard and played sports and I loved when my Dad and I were working or doing "guy" stuff.

I remember my Dad taking me to the Little League tryouts. I was in 5th grade and hadn't played ball since I quite tee-ball. We were both so excited to get there, he even bought me a new glove. I ran out on the field pumped and ready to show him how great I was. What actually happened was I sucked so bad it was a disgrace. This was not the same as tee-ball. I couldn't catch the ball. I couldn't hit the ball. I couldn't throw the ball, and I remember getting picked last for the Rugrats team. All the kids who didn't get picked for a team were placed on a team without a coach. I felt so ashamed walking back up to the truck when it was time to leave. I wanted to impress my Dad but instead I was a failure. Of course, those were my words not his. I suspect my Dad took me out for a Thrifty's ice cream cone to sooth the pain. He wasn't harsh or mean. Actually, he always has been a very kind-hearted person. Thinking back, I wanted to be his son so bad that I put a lot of pressure on our relationship. No matter how well I played sports, I was never going to be his son. I was his daughter. My Dad was in a winless situation too. He could have never done the right thing (in my young thinking) to make everything the way I wanted it.

I couldn't explain or comprehend how or why or what I wanted. I didn't even know what I wanted.

I tried so hard on that first Little League team. I was so driven and intense that I won an award for the most improved, and our team won the championship that year. Our coach ended up being the support I needed to come out of my shell. He fed my need to please and helped me show it on the field in the most innocently powerful and loving way. He was a kind but tough person and gave me the confidence and empowerment I needed. I think he was special to me because he treated me like a person, not a girl with cute blonde curls, but a powerful unstoppable human. He was a hulk-built African American man with beautiful dark skin. His wife was the assistant coach, a white blonde woman. During that time, the city I grew up in had mostly Mexican folks and a few white folks; that was it. Coach didn't fit in, just like me. He was black and I was a scrawny white "tomboy". He was amazing, kind and basically my superhero. He allowed me to thrive at sports, which gave me purpose. Those skills and that mindset got me through my childhood. In my mind, I could be a superhero too if I just gave everything I had. Sports served as an excellent place to let all of the real me out and let my light shine. I was intense on the field. When I had a tough day, I projected all of my frustrations and anger into the game. I was a force to deal with in my everyday life, yet on the field or in the game I was at peace. Life was hard only when I wasn't playing or practicing sports.

I still didn't have words to understand me but no one else in my life had the capacity to see me either — not the real me. If they did see the real me, they didn't have the capacity to like me, support me and love me. My family loved me and supported me the best way they knew how, but they just didn't "see" me. They saw what they understood me to be through my physical body. My Mom did try. She was the one who always let me have the "boys" toys and boy friends. She understood that I was a "tomboy".

That word again.

The word I was called by everyone my whole childhood.

Tomboy.

It made it okay for others to let me be me.

To leave me be.

"Yep she's just a Tomboy."

"She doesn't like dresses."

In first grade, I finally convinced my Mom to let me cut my hair off. It was really hard decision for my Mom because she loved my gorgeous locks. They were blonde and wild like a lion's mane. I was one of those people that had the hair everyone wants. But of course, true to form, the person having the "good" hair never wants it. I didn't want it for other reasons. That hair made me more like a girl and less like me. I hated it from the core of my soul. So, when Mom let me chop it, I felt free. I felt like me. I felt invincible. That night, we went to my Dad's softball game. I was on top of the world. I had that feeling you get when you know you are feeling good and looking good. Like when you have a new outfit for the first day of school. That "check me out and my new Vans" kind of feeling. My Dad's softball team was made up of friends and family. He played in leagues for most of his life. As I walked up to the field and bleachers full of people who loved me, I was happy and confident. Then one of my relatives loudly whispered, "Well now she really looks like a boy."

"Well now she really looks like a boy."

Boom!

There it was - the bomb!

Those words stung!

They reminded me what the world was really like.

They again reminded me,

"Don't you dare look or act different!"

"People notice and it's not okay."

I'm not ok.

It still stings. Think about that. Something that took seconds for someone to say stung me my entire life. From what I'm told, it wasn't obvious those things hurt me. I wasn't a depressed, sad, or weak kid. No, I took another route. I became stronger on the outside. I became tough and like a lion, and I would roar when attacked. However, I was a boiling volcano inside my fully grown 5'2" skinny little body. My mantra was, "Become crazier, louder, and scarier than them so they would leave me alone"… and it worked… most of the time.

When I was seven, we moved to a cabin outside of Los Angeles with my Mom, Dad, and two sisters. I loved my cabin life. It was the best thing that could have happened to me. I got to help my Dad with every chore you could possibly think of from stacking fire wood to digging ditches. I became the best helper anyone could ask for. I was so proud of myself. I felt normal and loved by my Dad. I finally felt as if he treated me as an equal and with respect. I am not saying that he didn't before, but I am saying I finally felt that I was equal to those other boys I had been jealous of before. Those were some of the best memories of my childhood — busting my butt working with my Pop. I never understood why my older sister never wanted to help or how she strategically planned to have wet nails every single time we asked for help. I never minded helping. I had my Dad fulfilling my need to fit in and be accepted. My Mom accepted me too by telling me I could do anything. She said it so many times I believed her. She would tell me I was special and that was a good thing. Although, she didn't really understand just how special I was. My sisters also accepted and loved me for me. They never questioned who I was or how I was. I was just me, the one who carried the firewood and helped Dad. My life at that point was rad and I loved it. I had so many adventures at our cabin, everything was amazing.

Then I became a girl...

Out of nowhere I turned into a girl — I mean a "real" girl! I couldn't hide it anymore. Not only that, but I was a "teenage" girl. Everything changed. It really was all a blur to me. I remember feeling weird and knowing I needed to fit in order to survive this. I told myself that I could do it. I could still be me. Not all of me but the part that people liked. The nice, kind, funny me — that me. I could be that person, at school I had many friends and was loyal to each of them. I was popular and loved that people liked me. I could do this, No problem! I would become boy crazy with pictures of Rob Lowe all over my room. Side note, I still think he's pretty. I tried to fit in, and I pushed anything else I felt down deep and drowned it inside of me. I could be the girl they wanted me to be or who I thought I was expected to be.

Then my Dad started treating me different. I'm not sure which came first (because my hormones triggered) and I started treating everyone different. I was mad about everything. I was mad this was happening to me. I was mad that I was being treated different. I was just mad. My jealousy returned. My Dad treated me differently from my male cousins, neighbors and even strangers. He treated me different now. Different like a girl. I don't think I'd ever been as heartbroken as I was when that happened. When I felt jealous, I would just get angry with him, and we would argue. Of course, we didn't argue about that exactly. I'm sure I made up another reason. We drifted apart. I kept playing sports through school and even a year of college. My Dad made every game — every single game — even the away games. He was there. By that time, I could care less that he was there. I was too caught up in my own "awesomeness". It was too hard for me to be close to him and not be his son. To feel less than hurt too much. I was reminded of something I didn't want to face. Although (truthfully) if he hadn't come to those games I would have been devastated. Either way, at this point, our relationship was pretty bruised and beaten. Don't get me wrong-my family wasn't mean or hurtful. They loved me and loved each other. I was just lost and I didn't know who I was or what I was going to do in my life. I felt pretty hopeless and scared.

Then, I realized I like girls. I would dream at night about a certain girl who was a friend of mine. When I'd wake I would try to fall back asleep so I could pretend I was a boy and we were in love. I would try so hard to go back to sleep, but I would finally have to get up again as me. I never told a soul about any of these feelings or those dreams. By the time I was 21, I knew I had to move away from home. In my mind, the city I lived in didn't allow "different" or gay people. I only saw people hating gays. I heard of people who killed themselves because they were gay and were hated. I thought about ending my life so I didn't have to be this way. I knew I couldn't do that. I made the decision I was going to live. So, I decided I needed to leave home. I needed to get out and see if I was still weird or different somewhere else. If I stayed, I would continue on a path of self-destruction. I met women that were gorgeous, feminine, and liked girls. They also liked me. That changed everything! I figured out I must be gay. I like them, they like me, when this happens people say you're gay. I thought, "I'm gay! I'm so gay." However, I couldn't face my family and friends with this truth, so I moved far away. I made new friends and a new life. I pretended I didn't care about what anyone thought. The truth was I did care. I just put my guard up to protect myself.

When I left for Seattle, I told my Mom I'd be back in a few months. I was gone for 19 years. I know now it broke her heart that I was gone so long. I would come back and visit and stay in contact. But, I mostly stayed away. I was too scared to be the real me. I was afraid that if I was the real me, I would not be loved by my family. When I visited back home I would bring my current girlfriend. I would, like my Aunt said, "Throw it in their faces". I guess I did do that. Again, I did what I always did. I thought if I'm braver, tougher and louder than my family is they can't hurt me. I used that strategy for many years. I was so good at it … until I wasn't. My "bigger, tougher, and louder" stopped working for me. I no longer wanted that aggression or angry interaction. It was very tiring being on the defense all of the time for over a decade. It was needed back when I was younger, but now it was just exhausting.

I also knew something else wasn't quite right within me. No matter how many amazing, kind, beautiful women I dated, something was off. I still knew there was more. I would look around for the answers in friends but never saw anyone I could relate to. I was still very different than my friends.

The pivotal moment that changed everything for me was when I was standing in that gas station in Seattle in 2011. Seattle usually drizzles — the kind of constant spray that keeps the ground wet but you don't need protection from. That day it was raging down like an angry river. Just gnarling out. I was standing in that rain with a black T-Shirt, black Dickies and black shoes. Rain flowed over my shaved head and over my face. My fists were clenched and begging to strike that old white man. For all of the other old, white, conservative, violent men that have come before him. How we got there is unimportant. The important fact was we were there standing at that gas station face to face. I wasn't afraid of him, and I was tired of being a victim. I ran up to him screaming "Let's go MutherFucker. Say it to my face. Come on. Hit me." Then something happened in his eyes that shook me. It snapped me awake and brought me out of the rage and into the present. So present that I could hear the attendant talking now. I thought, "Oh shit, what have I done?" I told her to call the police and that he was threatening me. He turned and jumped in his car and drove off.

I'm positive that I tried to take on a killer because he said he's, "…sick of little bitches like me." And the way he said those words… it was more than an idle threat. I felt ugly, defeated, embarrassed, and terrified. This was my rock bottom. I didn't even recognize myself anymore. Who was this angry violent raging person? I had reasons in the past for being that way, sure, but this? It wasn't me… not the real me. That real me was hard to see anymore, and it scared me. I'm not sure at the time what shook me more — the serial killer dude or what I would have done to him.

That was my moment. As I walked back to my jeep in the middle of the street, door open, rain pouring down, I knew I had to go and admit what I did. I had to tell Nancy, my Therapist, I slipped. I didn't use the counting technique or breathing trick. I didn't stop to think or walk away. I worked so hard every week for a year at therapy. Now, here I was again lashing out. I had humiliated myself again. I had to tell Nancy, but really, I had to hear myself say it. Admit I did that. I did it. But I'm a kind, loving, gentle person; at least I used to be. Who am I now? Where did I go? I knew I needed to change. Things had become urgent for me — even life threatening. I had a choice of course, keep this path and ruin my life or face my shit. My life depended on it.

I was done. I was no longer going to take it. From others or myself. I couldn't. I told Nancy I was ready to face it-change-handle-deal whatever it took to fix me. I chose me. I dedicated my time and energy to this work. I call it "walk through the mud". I could no longer avoid it. I needed to get dirty and walk right through it. So, I did. I faced what I had avoided. I invested in me, and it was the best investment I ever made.

Then the time came that I had dreaded.

It was time to say it out loud, the thing that I couldn't face my entire life. The thing I couldn't avoid any longer. Once I said it, I was in it. I was making the decision to do this. I knew I needed to tell people, specifically my friends and family. After I told them, they may decide they don't love me anymore because of this. I called my Mom to tell her the thing that would change both of our lives in that moment forever. I remember the conversation clearly. I suspect it was a blur for her.

It went something like this:

"Mom, I need you to listen. I have to tell you something big. I need you to support me. Mom, I have been brave, tough and stood up for myself over these past 15 years. I didn't need you to defend me. I defended myself. But this I can't do alone. This I 'need' you for. I need you to be momma bear and defend and support me. I can't live through this without you. Don't tell Dad."

She sounded scared but said yes she would support me.

Then I told her. I didn't want it to be true but it was. I lived 37 years this way and couldn't take it anymore and I was going to do something about it.

I decided to change my gender.

All of these years of trying to figure out why I wasn't quite right. Why I hurt so much. I told her, and then I hit the floor crying, broken, but free. It was the hardest moment of my life, and my Mom stood up to the challenge. The biggest challenge I had faced as her kid, and by far the biggest challenge she faced as a Mom. I wonder what was harder, losing my brother at birth or losing her daughter at 37. I'll have to ask her that when I see her; when I can hug her, and tell her I love her.

I was terrified to go home to California and see my Dad. One day in my sister's house in Seattle, I told her I was never going back to California. That I couldn't face the family. I was terrified and I didn't have the strength to do it. I loved them so much but they were kryptonite and I needed to be Superman right now. I couldn't do it. She quickly replied, "Well, that's not going to happen." And she immediately bought two tickets to L.A. She flew with me, held my hand, and supported me every second. I don't remember her talking much, she was just a supportive shadow. She and I both knew I needed my family to see my physical changes along this journey, so it wasn't so shocking at the end result. When I got to my parent's house my Dad was awkward and his quiet self. He went out back to smoke so I followed him. We sat in silence for a while. Then he said calmly, "I'm never going to call you anything other than Julie. You're my daughter. I named you. I love you, but I'm never going to call you anything other than Julie."

Inside I was crushed. I was that kid again getting laughed at out on the field, and my Dad wasn't standing up for me. He was too afraid of what people would think. He didn't have the courage to stand up for me. That's what I thought, but what I said was, "Okay Dad." Then I said, "But after a while it will get pretty awkward for people in public." He didn't get my joke. Instead he said, "Your Mom thought we were going to fight." When I was a teenager, we argued all the time, until my Mom gave us both a talking to. She let us know we will never fight again. After that, Dad gave me code words if we get heated. His big secret code was the peace sign. When he puts his two fingers up that's supposed to mean "Time-out" or something. On the porch, my Dad finished his cigarette and said, "I told your Mom we wouldn't fight." Then, he asked if I was mad at him. I said, "Dad, I didn't expect anything else than what you're capable of. I'm not mad at you." I tried to reach him one more time by saying, "Dad, how would you feel if you were born with boobs?" Those questions were more than he could take. He threw his hands in the air and dropped his head. So, I said, "Do you remember when I was a kid and all the work we did? How much I helped?" He'd reached his capacity, so I let it go. We went back inside and told each other we loved each other. It's funny because ending with "but I love you" seems sweet and loving. But really it was "I love you… conditionally." That is a hard reality to face.

In the end, I knew it would take my Dad some time. I knew my Mom would have a lot of leg work and translating to do to get this through to him. They have been together since the 9th grade. They are each other's "only". After a few years of regularly visiting my family with the hormone changes and transition taking effect on my body, I decided to move back to California. I was about an hour from my parent's house living near the beach. I was ready to leave Seattle and join the beach life. Over the next few years I visited my family now and again. It wasn't ever easy hearing the "she" pronouns or my old name being called. I made a pact with myself that I would never get upset with someone for messing up my gender when speaking to me or about me, especially family. Early in my transition an overzealous "friend" shamed my sister Tami for making a mistake on my gender. This person gave me a gift when she did that. I knew immediately my family and friends would never experience that shame again. That experience taught me to give patience and room for people to make pronoun mistakes. I also learned one of the most valuable lessons during those early days, "I can be mad about everything or I could just not be mad." I could choose to handle this in a different way. The moment my sister was berated, I jumped in and made it clear to everyone, including my sister, that I would never be upset. That it was okay to mess up, and that I loved her. It was actually life changing for me. I gave people room. I also gave myself some room. For me, I needed to give room, space, patience, and love. I do not like to feel embarrassed, and I cannot stand for anyone else to be either. That works most of the time unless someone is, of course, not trying. For the first few years, I would come around the family, and some people would call me Drew, others would make mistakes, and some wouldn't try at all. At least it seemed they didn't try. I have never had more patience than I have during this time of my life.

My mantra was, "Watered, Rested, and Fed. It takes patience to be me."

I remember about three years into my transition I was at our family business. It was closing after 60 years in business. It was a stressful time, and my parents were scared about their future. I had been coming around for weeks helping with the cleanup. That day, several family members were in town. Most of them were calling me Julie or She. It was similar to a cringe-worthy holiday with too many family members in one place. Up until this day, I only had a few interactions with a couple family members at a time. But this day it was too many people and too much. The stress of the Family business closing and me being there was overwhelming. One cousin introduced me as Drew also known as Julie. I didn't lose it, I simply turned to the person and said, "Hi, please call me Drew." That day my Dad was also calling me Julie and She. I finally looked at my Mom and said, "I'm leaving. I can't do this anymore. I love you, but I can't be here. You all aren't even trying, and Dad isn't at all. Mom, I'm leaving and you all don't get to keep me anymore. Dad doesn't get to keep me."

She said, "I'll handle it", and I left.

A few days later, my Dad called me.

"Drew" he said.

I said "Yea."

"Did you hear me? I said, Drew."

"Yea, Dad I heard you."

"Well, I talked with your Mom, and I'm going to try. I'm going to try, but I'll probably mess up so we'll have a code word."

I interrupted and said, "Dad, look you don't see me. You don't respect me." He got quiet. I usually would be yelling at this point or going the other way out of discomfort saying, "It's ok Dad. It's ok." Not this time. I kept up with a calm serious voice. I could hear my mentor saying, "Calm assertive energy" in my ear. I kept on, "All I've ever wanted was for you to love me. You give your love away easy to any guy who comes around — anyone. Some of which are assholes, felons, or whatever. You give them respect, but me, nope. You don't see me. Do you know what it's like to not be seen? No, Dad it's not okay anymore." It got quiet. He said, "Well your Mom reminded me about when you were a kid, about all the times you helped me and all the things we did together. I forgot about all of that." I said "Yea Dad, I was like a son to you."

I don't remember what else we said. This was the hardest yet easiest conversation I had ever had with him. Maybe because I wasn't angry with him. I was hurt but not mad at him. I am so grateful for that conversation. I'm so proud of both of us for having it. I knew when I had that first conversation on the porch with him that it would take time. I knew my Mom would be the key to his understanding. When our phone conversation ended, I knew I still needed to give him love and support because now he was trying. I also realized that this wasn't easy for him, but he was going to try. That's all I wanted from any of them — to try. To love me and to try. I never expect anyone who isn't going through this to understand. I barely understood. I couldn't expect anyone else to. I just wanted to be loved, supported and for them to give loving effort. My 89-year-old paternal Grandma got it right away and jumped on board. I knew it was possible; they just had to want to do it.

What I learned about my experience so far is my part in it. That this wasn't just something I went through. We all are going through something. I can't expect someone to meet me where I am if they haven't met themselves where they are. They can only give what they are capable and willing to give. I can choose if that's enough or not, but I get to choose. In the last two years, my parents have been there for me through my heart break with my relationship ending, my success, and my travel. They support and love me unconditionally. I taught them how to sell on eBay and they recreated their future. We have a better relationship than we have ever had my entire life. I owe that to all of us trying to meet each other where we are today. Not where I want them to be or how I want them to be, but where they are. They do the same for me. It's an amazing feeling being accepted and loved for who you are today.

I can't imagine how hard this has been for my parents. I expected a lot from them and they have stood up to the task. It took them time, but they are doing it. I'm so proud of them and their unconditional love. This is what it looks like and feels like. They did the best they could with what they knew, and when they knew better they did better. I was also there to remind them. I don't regret my childhood or hold bitterness toward my parents or anyone else for that matter. What I experienced created who I am. I feel lucky to be me. If I had been born any other way, I wouldn't be me and I love myself. I am proud of myself for stepping into my bigger life. For taking the steps and path to change my gender. For becoming the authentic me and dedicating myself to become the best version of me every day. It has taken more strength, courage, and patience than I imagined. It was worth it. It is still worth it. This was the scariest thing I avoided most of my life. I didn't think I could do it or what "it" would turn out to be. Being my most authentic brave self is the best gift I could have ever given myself. It was my soul's purpose, and now I'm free.

ABOUT DREW BENSEN

Entrepreneur
Author-Public Speaker
Empowerment Coach
Full-Time RV Traveler Transgender Man

Drew lives full time in his Winnebago traveling North America. He considers himself an innate Entrepreneur who loves public speaking and living his most authentic life. He is also a transgender man (born female at birth), and an inspirational Coach. Drew is a co-author in the book, "Positive Minded People", and spends most of his time on Southern California beaches with his dog Ralphie.

DrewBensen.com

Instagram
https://Instagram.com/PositivelyRealLife

CHAPTER 9

THE POSITIVE EXPERIENCE OF PAIN

Calvin Witcher

Does anyone really care about positivity anyway? I know that people say we should care. But, do we care at our core about positivity? Perhaps we only care about the results of positivity. I used to think that positivity was this bliss-filled and burden-free experience. Boy, have I grown to think differently. Positivity, as I have learned, is consistent contentment through one's intended outcome. I believe that some of us learn the lessons of life through tragedy and others through triumphs. In these circumstances, both, the one that experiences tragedy and the one that experiences triumph, have a positive experience. The positive experience, or intended outcome, can be learned by both individuals. For many people, positivity is simply not experiencing pain. For me however, positivity is about understanding that sometimes pain is the positive experience. And, oftentimes, pain doesn't just occur through situations but through specific people. For me, learning how to be peaceful and positive in the midst of pain and persecution has been the ultimate journey of my life. Embracing the positive experience of pain has been a life work. So, how exactly did I come to this understanding?

Well, let's go for a journey down memory lane. This is my story.

It all started in Virginia. The motto of my town was (and still is), "Ain't no big thang, but it's growing"; at least, that's what the sign displayed as you entered town. Well, there was growth alright. Most of the areas of growth that I experienced, or at least perceived, were growth in frustration, discrimination, and hostility. And, other times it was growth in sheer complacency. At least that's what it looked like at a glance. Don't get me wrong. I actually loved my town and still do. But, being "different," in a town that seemed to stay the same was quite the challenge.

My earliest memories of myself are intimately and intrinsically linked to one point, or shall I say one person… my grandmother. Even though I lived with my mother, and she did an excellent job raising me as a single parent, my grandmother had the most significant influence on my spiritual life. Since my life has always revolved around spirituality, she made the most impact on me.

I have fond memories of my times with my grandmother. I remember spending a lot of weekends and summers with her, especially after my grandfather died. I didn't know him too well, but from what I can remember, he was a hard worker that took care of his family. I remember him being a quiet and stable man. You know the type; he was the man you could always depend on and was a rock for his family. When he passed, it affected my grandmother dramatically. While I'm not sure to what extent, I do know that my connection with my grandmother increased. It could have been because I was around her more than other family members and her friends during this time. It could be that my grandmother had a shift in priorities. I'm sure most of her married life was focused on her faith, her family, and specifically her husband. At this point, her children were all grown and had their own homes and families. It's interesting to note that my grandfather's passing is the first death I remember. Death is a mysterious phenomenon, in that, someone is here with us today and gone the next. It's instant transformation. That which we have known suddenly becomes the unknown. I've found that life changes carry a similar mission; situations encourage us to push beyond our comfort zone into other unfamiliar territories that hopefully are more fulfilling for us. Living without my grandfather was definitely a new territory for my grandmother and even me.

There were nights that my grandmother would cry herself to sleep or simply not sleep at all. Whenever I asked how she was doing or if I could get her anything, she would simply reply, "Pretty, I'm ok." She called everyone "Pretty". That was her trademark word. That one word carried worlds of experiences with it that still remain undiscovered.

In those days, following my grandfather's passing, I learned to carry the weight of more responsibility. It wasn't necessarily an inconvenience; it was just more obvious all the work that he contributed to the family now that he was gone. Some of this "work" manifested as emotional support, and in other ways, it was helping around the house. I helped my grandmother tend the garden, wash clothes (by hand on a washing board), gather water from the well, chop wood for the fire, chase moccasin snakes out of the house, boil water for cleaning, feed the dogs, tend the garden, and much more. I also went grocery shopping with my grandmother, which usually meant going to multiple stores for different products; Amos' for this, Leena Blair's for that, Old Dutch for other things, and so on.

During the week, I went to work with my grandmother. She didn't have conventional employment. She took care of "the white folks". This wasn't a racist position, but it was a role position. It was just the way things were at that time. She was black and they were white. In our community in Virginia, this distinction was very well known and practiced. So, yes, my grandmother took care of "the white folks". She cleaned their houses, washed their clothes, cared for their children, cooked for them, and basically whatever else they needed. I was present for the entire process. May I also add this — from my experience, my grandmother never neglected me, her family, her faith, or her personal responsibilities. I thought she juggled these roles quite well considering her age and the circumstances. I also never heard her complain about her life and she was a model example of positivity. Either way, it was interesting going with my grandma to work. I never remember an unkind word or behavior towards me or her but I did "know my place". I was allowed to play outside. I was permitted to be in one small room on the side of the house but not permitted to be in other parts of the main house simply because I was black. I was the son of "the help". Circumstances like this definitely made me stay in line and "know my place" in my community. To this day, I still don't remember where I went to the bathroom (possibly outside in the field). Some of my fondest memories with my grandmother come from this time in life. I witnessed her living in grace, dignity, and with a spirit of understanding. Yes, I remember her having times of frustration, but I never remember her living in fear or with anger at any point in her life.

On Sundays, I went to church with my grandmother. It was an old country church on a winding back road a few miles away from my grandma's house. It had one entrance into the church, and there was only a large meeting room and one bathroom. From what I understand, this was the church where she discovered Jesus, had become "saved from her sins", and the only church she was ever a member. That church was Burning Bush Pentecostal Holiness Church. The membership was small, mostly consisting of a few families, and it was here that I had my first encounters with the Spirit of God (as we called "Him"). At the time, we would never think of considering God anything other than male. That house-turned-church truly made an impact in my spiritual development. While there was never more than a handful of members present, it was here that I was healed of asthma, and later, eczema.

Being healed of asthma and eczema was no small matter. My childhood was colored with frequent visits to the emergency room and doctor's office. I carried an inhaler with me at all times and used my nebulizer treatments often. I had limited physical activities due to this breathing disorder. My eczema consumed a lot of my daily and nightly routine. During the day, I had to ensure my body stayed moisturized to prevent dry skin. The eczema covered my head down to my feet. Whenever I experienced dry skin, I would scratch profusely, and for a young child like me, it was seemingly uncontrollable. During the nights, my mother would bathe me from head-to-toe with baby oil and lotion, then wrap my feet and hands with Saran Wrap in order to retain the moisture, and then secure my hands and feet with socks. This nightly ritual was observed because I would scratch to the point of bleeding and my bed sheets would be colored with blood and soaked in sweat every morning. So, when I say "healed", I don't mean I outgrew these diseases. I remember the service at my grandmother's church where I walked in with eczema and walked out free and clear as if I never had the disease at all. It was quite the experience.

When I wasn't with my grandmother, either at work, church, or her home, I was at home with my Mom.

My Mom is a strong woman and was a single parent raising a strong-willed, and spiritually sensitive boy. My grandmother taught me how to be a strong spiritual person and my mother taught me to be a strong and confident young man. They did an excellent job, and for this, I am eternally grateful.

Don't get me wrong, my mother was instrumental in my spiritual life too, but in a different way. She introduced a more structured side of religion to me through the Baptist faith which was quite different from the free flowing and spirited Pentecostalism of my grandmother. Now, with that structure often came inflexible ideologies, which affected me in the most interesting ways. I was a peculiar child to say the least. I wore thick "coke bottle glasses"; I was a loner; my version of fun was going to church and studying the Bible; I was physically sick a lot; I lived in low-income housing (which we called the projects); and oh, did I mention – I was gay. Well, I still am gay but that's not the point right now.

I remember the countless times being called derogatory names, protecting myself from bullies, having my property destroyed, and this occurred in my community, at school, and even in church. Church members seemed to be the worst at times, especially since spirituality is where I felt most "at home".

My nickname in church was "Wiz Kid" because I asked too many questions or oftentimes had annoying responses to religious statements that were made. I thought I was a rationally thinking student simply seeking answers to my faith. For example, "God created mankind in his image..." I would simply inquire, "If God created mankind, then who/what created God?" Seems like a good question. One of my favorite scriptures at the time was, "God is a Spirit, and they that worship HIM must worship HIM in spirit and in truth." "So, I'm curious Sunday School teacher, last week you said, 'The spirit has no gender.' But, if God is a Spirit, why do we always say *he*; why not *she* or *it*?" I was usually met with some snarky statement that my thoughts were crazy and borderline disrespectful. How dare I call God, IT.

For all intents and purposes, my spiritual community and natural life was far from "normal" and considering the circumstances, I never considered these positive experiences.

To make things more interesting, my spiritual experiences (outside of church) were even more entertaining.

At an early age, around eight years old I believe, I started noticing "weird" things happening to me and around me... and in me. And, by weird, I mean I started hearing voices throughout the day and night. Well, to be accurate, it started with hearing things, then seeing things, then knowing things, then feeling things, and then the manifestations occurred.

For a long time, I just thought the voices were the inevitable effect of watching too many scary movies before going to bed at night. I was experiencing what many parents had warned their children of for generations. "Don't watch scary movies before bedtime or you'll have nightmares." At this point, the voices didn't feel like a nightmare; it was more of a nuisance than anything else. The voices went from unrecognizable whispers, to full blown audible and coherent conversations. For the longest time, I thought I wasn't getting enough sleep, but after getting plenty of rest, the internal whispers grew into external dialogues between me and "the others". "The others" seemed like a fitting name considering they never formally introduced themselves. At the beginning, the voices were strangers, but for a young boy who didn't fit in anywhere, they quickly became my closest friends. It's interesting what you gravitate to when you're lacking in other areas. Now, don't get me wrong. I have did have good friends growing up, but I always knew I was different.

"The others" weren't really saying anything specific or life changing. Rather, they were just having conversation and, mostly, just saying phrases like, "How are you?", "Where are you going?", "Why are you doing that?", "You think we're not real?", "We're more real than you are!", and so on.

The "weird" things continued but simultaneously splintered into the next two categories; I started seeing things and knowing things, often before they occurred. I began to see events in my dreams and sometimes during the day while I was fully awake. For example, I could see what a teacher would wear to school that day; word-for-word conversations I would have with friends, car accidents, and so on. Where the seeing stopped, the knowing picked up and seemed to give me the story of the events I was seeing. It was almost like a narrator giving a detailed account of every scene I saw.

Next, the feelings started. This was probably the most annoying and agonizing stage because now I started feeling everything. I mean EVERY THING. I could feel the next movement of the wind; I could feel the emotion behind every conversation; I could feel the joy of the artist when listening to music on the radio; I felt the collective emotions of groups in school, and I could feel the sadness of a tree that had just lost a branch. Sometimes the feelings weren't just emotional but also physical. I started feeling the crushed ribs of a squirrel that had just been run over by a passing car, the shortness of breath of the athlete running track at school, and all of this just continued day after day.

After the feelings came the manifestations. This is where things got real. The manifestations mostly happened at night. It started with little things like me placing an item on my dresser and leaving the room and then that item was gone or moved to a different location. I know this wasn't my mother because I would give her little "tests", and many times she was not home when the events occurred. When she was home, I would ask my mother if she personally moved "something" in my room but I wouldn't tell her what the "something" was. Depending on her answer, I would know if she moved the correct object or not. Sometimes, I would place items in hard to reach places where it would be highly unlikely for her to come in contact with the object. Lo and behold, even those objects were moved. These are some of the strategies I used to better understand the moving manifestations and how I proved my mother had nothing to do with them. I also remember times where I was lying in bed and felt a breeze rush in the room despite the windows and doors being closed. Sometimes, I saw faint silhouettes in the corner of my room. As I was walking around the house, doors would open and close on their own, lights would flicker, and the radio and television would come on and off by themselves.

These events, and many more, continued to increase over time and remain even until today. I went through a large majority of my childhood angry and aggressive simply because I had no one to talk to. I had little-to-no understanding of what was happening. I would blow up over "little things" (as they seemed to others) but they were huge things that often caused me unspeakable pain. There were times I simply felt abandoned on the earth without a soul to confide in. This personal pain continued. And honestly, It just didn't feel fair.

While what was happening to me was scary, I also felt significant, and in an odd sense, empowered. I didn't know anyone else who had experiences like this. Over the years, I learned to cherish those moments as special gifts from God. I never really talked about it to my pastor and members of the church because I knew it would not be received well. I didn't discuss it with family either because I didn't see anything beneficial coming from it. I went through life as "normal" as I could.

This happened for years. I learned how to navigate my spiritual experiences through trial and error.

Eventually, I channeled my passion for my "secret gifts" into something that would be more readily acceptable to my community — music. I played the saxophone and eventually learned to play piano. Playing the piano turned out to be quite the useful skill because I was really good at it. Also, our church needed a pianist for Sunday services around the same time. We did have one, but because of his "sin", he was asked to leave the church. What was his sin? He had a baby out of wedlock — and they let EVERYONE know it. I remember that he HAD to appear in front of the entire church one Sunday, admit his sin, and inform everyone that he would no longer be the musician for the church. As I recall, he never came to church again (at least our church that is). And really, who could blame him? It was the most humiliating experience I had ever witnessed and definitely the most memorable. When you witness something like this in church, one of the first things you think is, "This will never happen to me. I need to make sure I protect myself from situations and people like this."

Don't get me wrong, everyone quickly moved on past this public display of disgrace. And now with the former pianist out of the way, I took the lead. I really enjoyed playing piano for a long time because I was able to rewrite some of my "church image". I went from being the "know it all and arrogant little boy" to an "talented and anointed young man". That kind of role reversal will boost anyone's ego. I took the new persona and ran with it, pouring my heart and soul into church music at every chance I got. But, that's not all I was doing at the time. I travelled with my pastor and church to other meetings. I served as Assistant Choir Director and Worship Leader. I was the Youth President, and at one time a Youth Deacon. Life was pretty darn good from my perspective.

No one knew about all of the more significant spiritual experiences that were still happening, but on the surface, I was a rising star. And at the time, that's what mattered most.

My popularity didn't just increase at church, but it also increased at school. I traded my "coke bottle glasses" for contacts. I changed my attitude and my attire, and quickly amassed a new set of "friends" and with it, influence. Those were very powerful and pivotal moments in my life because I began to realize how little shifts had a massive impact and an enormous impact with me and others.

As the years progressed on, I became more settled "in my skin", my spiritual experiences, and the society that surrounded me. I had made it. I was validated. I was victorious. I was free.

Life wasn't perfect by any means. During my high school years, I lost dear friends that I loved. I also had back surgery for scoliosis which greatly impacted my everyday life. Despite these things, life was still in an upswing.

I graduated from high school and was voted "Most Musical" by my senior class. The musical baton was being passed to another pianist at my church. I was accepted into a private college in Bristol, VA and in a few months, I would have a new residence. Life as I had known it was in a state of transition and I welcomed every change.

When the time came to start my freshmen year of school, my Mom happily navigated the scenic route from Gretna to Bristol to help me settle in on my new home for the next few years. College was a great experience and a chance to start over. No one knew me; however, I was still in the process of knowing who I really was. I wasn't a big fan of going to classes though. When I was in the science lab or in Political Science class, all I could think about was ministry and spirituality. As the days went on, my desires for something "other than school" increased, while my motivation for college and grades decreased.

Over the span of time, I had learned to accept my gifts and identify them for what they were. I learned to validate myself and my experiences. Even though I didn't public express my passion for my spiritual gifts, I still affirmed my truth to myself.

I could hear things – I was a Channeler and Medium.

I could see things – I was a Prophet.

I could know things – I was a Psychic.

I could feel things – I was an Empath.

I could effect change – I was a Shaman.

I didn't fully understand everything about myself but, as time went on, I learned to embrace these realities more fully.

While in college, I got connected with two churches in the area and began operating in one of my roles as a Prophet to those ministries. It was a really good time. I wasn't "officially" a member of those churches, but the Pastors trusted the "call on my life" and the evidence of my gift that they had experienced as being from God.

Things were slowly going in the direction I wanted. I never really LOVED school, so I devoted more time to ministry. My devotion to my spiritual journey was quickly paying off.

I remember leaving work one night to go to a local Assemblies of God church that I had been to previously. They were having a revival and a Prophet was the guest minister – well, a Prophetess to be exact. I was in need of a good recharge from the week, and it had been a while since I had been around a female prophet. Something happened at work and I got out extremely late; so late that I considered not going because I assumed the church service was already finished. Something inside me encouraged me to go anyway so I went. As I suspected, the service was coming to a close and I barely made it. I quietly snuck in the sanctuary, as to not disturb the service, and I sat down somewhere in the back of the church.

Almost immediately after sitting down, the Prophetess yelled out from the front, "Hey you! The person that just came in the door. Come here. Yes, you in the back." I was the only person that had just entered the church, but I still looked around to confirm my sneaking suspicion that she was talking to me. She began prophesying to me about my destiny as a Prophet and how she was told by Spirit to mentor me throughout the process.

The months following that experience led me to quit my job, leave school, and relocate to South Carolina to be personally mentored by the Prophetess.

I was excited. Life was good. Until it wasn't.

I failed to mention earlier that a young man I knew from back home moved to Bristol to help me with my ministry. He said, "I feel led by God to work with you". At the time, I was elated. My ministry was expanding and my team was growing. He followed me and worked with me for quite a while.

In the middle of my big move to South Carolina, he had a moment of honesty with one of the Pastors that I knew. He told them that he moved to be with me because he was in love with me. He confessed to them that he had sexual feelings towards me. Of course, I knew nothing about this and definitely wouldn't have made this public because I knew the results that would ensue. After all, I never forgot our former pianist's fall from grace, and I vowed that would never be me.

Now, it WAS me.

How everything unfolded after his confession seemed like a blur. From what I understand, he only told one pastor, but that often means nothing in the religious community. Conversations in the church travel fast and gossip even faster. Even though I never confessed to anything, I was guilty by association. Consequently, everyone immediately assumed I was gay (which was true but undisclosed) and they started disassociating from me.

I thought things would settle down, but they didn't. I had been in South Carolina for quite a while by this time. Things had grown quiet, so I was hoping that everything had finally finished. I knew that many of my prior connections before moving had been crippled (to say the least) but all was well because I was in a new state and had the chance to start over.

Boy, was I wrong about that.

News eventually travelled to my ministry affiliation in South Carolina. This was probably the most uncomfortable conversation I ever had. I was living in the Prophetess' former home and also working with her in ministry. When she confronted me about the situation, of course, I told her I had nothing to do with the young man. His feelings were his own, and I didn't know he was gay. I don't remember if she asked me if I was gay or not and, honestly, I don't remember what I said. I do know that ministry was the only priority, so I would have said whatever I needed to in order to protect my path.

As much as I tried to convince her of my truth and worth, it just wasn't enough. She believed the word of the other Pastors and that she couldn't be associated with a potential scandal like this. And just like that...I was without a community (just like our former piano player back home).

It was an interesting time.

It was a memorable day.

It was a lonely night.

It was interesting because as gifted and as spiritually aware that I was, I couldn't sense it or see this ever happening to me. As a Prophet and Psychic, I could tell exactly where people were in their life and what was to come, but in my own life there was merely silence and darkness. In a weird and naïve sort of way, I felt invincible. I felt my love of God, my hunger for spiritual truths, and my commitment to the greater cause was enough. I found out that it wasn't.

It was memorable because it was one of those defining moments in life that changes everything. It was my phoenix experience. It was my great awakening. It was my salvation experience. I was being born again. But this new life was preceded by an agonizing death with eyes wide open, viewing the entire experience, as I experienced every moment of pain. I saw my world collapse. In that moment, I simply stood still and waited to be created anew.

It was a lonely night. I had spent over twenty years being gay and hiding my sexuality. I had ministered in several states and within countless churches. I had dedicated my time and a hell of a lot of money to building the "kingdom of God". There were times that I cursed God and abandoned church altogether out of the frustrations and injustices I saw. At one stage in my life, I was a mean, cold, arrogant, and an aggressive little boy. Despite all of that, I always felt the presence, power, and the person of God. But not this night.

Yes, this night was a lonely night; one that seemed to last an eternity. Maybe this was hell. If it was, it made a lot of sense. If this was hell, then I guess I deserved it.

When you're in hell, words like peace and positivity have entirely different meanings. However, when you're in a state of contentment, those same words of peace and positivity now appear as inevitable byproducts of your present blissful experience. Peace and positivity, in times of change, challenge, and crisis, seem like luxuries that you will never be able to afford.

I was alone. After all these years, and after everything I had done, now God had finally abandoned me. I was on my own.

I remember the moment all too well.

I stood alone in the cold kitchen of this rented house, bare feet securing my place on the ground that seemingly was being shaken underneath me, and I stared out of the window into the open sky hoping my desperation would pierce the soul of the darkness. As I gazed out of the window, my spiritual senses began to awaken and I could feel the evil of what happened to me surrounding me. I felt the darkness filling the empty space behind me.

I remained still; tear after tear moving from cheek to counter.

I turned around, and with every ounce of faith and hope remaining in me, I made this affirmation. I MAY FEEL ALONE BUT I AM NOT ALONE. I HAVE NEVER BEEN ALONE. I WILL NEVER BE ALONE. GOD IS WITH ME, HAS ALWAYS BEEN WITH ME, AND WILL FOREVER BE WITH ME. WE ARE IN THIS TOGETHER.

I then made this commitment to God and also to myself. I said everything aloud so I could hear my own confessions and the power it embodied. I said, "Since I get to start over, then I make these two promises. For starters, I will never do to others what was done to me. And next, I will explore my spiritual path in a way that is authentic and true to me. Period." And, those are the promises I have lived by ever since that moment.

Fast forward to today, at the time of writing this chapter, despite everything that has ever happened to me, life is better than good. I'm married to my husband of fourteen years and we have four children. We live in a beautiful community, surrounded by lakes and rivers. I have a beautiful spiritual community, online and in-person, that enjoy my teachings and my spiritual work. I am a life coach and spiritual mentor and enjoy the clients I'm privileged to work with. I travel across the nation expressing my gifts as a prophet, teacher, shaman, and everything in between. I share my gifts to individuals, groups, churches, spiritual centers, and various organizations. Because of what I went through with my college and church experiences, and because of the impeccable character and example of my grandmother, I help countless individuals that have experienced similar painful moments just like me. Thankfully, I am better equipped to help others heal, and I'm more sympathetic to their needs. Looking back, my pain was the best thing to ever happen to me because it was the catalyst to the confident life I now experience.

Through these excursions on the journey of my life, I've discovered new ways to invent and engineer my way into positivity. The secret is learning how to be at peace with all people, especially yourself. You must also learn to be at peace with the pain of your experiences. Your pain can produce something powerful in and through you. I know it may sound weird, but learn to be at peace with the painful times in your life. Peace, I think, is the prized possession that my grandmother held dear to her heart, and evangelistically proclaimed countless times throughout her life. She would often quote her favorite scripture from Hebrews 12:14, "Follow peace with all men, and holiness without which will no one see the Lord". Inner peace is an intrinsic, intimate, and eternal work. Never take the work for granted. It's impossible to embrace a positive experience when you're not at peace with the person you are or the position you're in. Pain can often blind us from the purpose of our path. Resist the temptation to avoid painful moments in your life. Pain could be the best thing to ever happen to you. Your pain provides the growth you experience, and positivity is the gain you earn for the losses you suffered along the way.

Oftentimes, when you lose your closest people, sacred philosophies, and valuable possessions, it is your persistence to remain positive that keeps you sane and stable in uncertain times. As I have embraced this knowing in my life, I have discovered that I can be all of who I am without choosing one over the other, and without the fear of complete and utter loss. Any perceived setback is only a temporary adjustment and realignment to get you back in the direction of your heart's desire. Just because you say, "Yes" to one thing, doesn't mean it's a "No" to everything else.

Yes, some things take time. Yes, bad things happen. Yes, hard times will come. And good times come too. The sun will rise and overpower your darkest night. You will be all you're meant to be and you may lose who you thought you had to be in the process. All things work together for your highest good, despite if it feels good or not.

As the world continues to evolve, I've learned to adjust my perspectives on life as needed. This perpetual state of prepared positivity is simply another transition along my life of transformation. I've learned that part of the human experience is confidently confessing your truth and navigating other people's responses and the consequences along the way. I've learned that though one thing may end in a season of your life, it is ultimately not the end of your story or your soul's satisfaction.

If you're in a difficult season of your life, I'm here to remind you of several things. You are not alone on this journey of your life. I understand you may be lonely right now, but eventually this cycle will change, just as sure as winter turns into spring. The pain you are experiencing has a purpose that time will ultimately verify.

You're not weird. Though things don't make sense right now, in time, you'll understand exactly why you are made the way you are. Just give it time. Don't give up on yourself. You owe it to yourself and your future to weather this storm. Accessing your internal power is only a few perspectives away. Keep moving forward as your soul leads you on. One day you'll be thankful that you did.

While this is only part of my story, it is *my story*. And, you have one too. While I've had my moments of pain, it has empowered healthier perspectives and produced positive moments in my life.

What will your story be? Don't allow your pain to put your life on pause. Pursue your life with greater purpose like never before.

Thank you for taking this journey with me. Now, the world is waiting to be inspired by your life.

ABOUT CALVIN WITCHER

As an internationally recognized Prophet, Calvin is here to set forth universal harmony. His spiritual mandate is to see, speak, and translate from the Spirit realm to this physical world. Prophet Calvin brings God's messages to humanity through powerful teaching and training, allowing non-traditional followers to hear the divine voice of hope.

Calvin, his products, and programs have been featured on Success Magazine, iTunes Top 30 spiritual video podcasts, Barnes & Nobles, and Amazon.com, just to name a few.

With a faith, undaunted by the task at hand, this husband, father, and mentor is the prophetic voice to a progressive generation. Today, as the Founder and proclaimer of Transitions Philosophy, he continues to fulfill his mission to radically heal and transform lives.

CalvinWitcher.com

For more information on philosophy, please visit
Transitionism.com

Conclusion

Thank you for experiencing the journey of this book with us. It is our hope that these stories helped enrich your life. May these stories serve as a resource for you to lean on in your challenging times.

We believe you have the power to create the life you want and we hope our stories served as a reminder of that fact.

We did it and so can you.

Made in the USA
Columbia, SC
01 December 2017